pray
a word for
hope

editors of guideposts

Pray a Word for Hope

Published by Guideposts Books & Inspirational Media, 100 Reserve Road, Suite E200, Danbury, CT 06810
Guideposts.org

Copyright © 2023 by Guideposts. All rights reserved.

This book, or parts thereof, may not be reproduced, stored in a retrieval system, or transmitted in any form or by any means, electronic, mechanical, photocopying, recording or otherwise, without the written permission of the publisher.

ISBN-13: 978-1-959634-00-3 (hardcover)
ISBN-13: 978-1-959634-09-6 (EPUB)
ISBN-13: 978-1-949634-08-9 (EPDF)

Cover and interior design by Serena Fox, Bean Inc.
Cover photo by Comussu, © Shutterstock
Typeset by Aptara, Inc.

Printed and bound in the United States of America
10 9 8 7 6 5 4 3 2 1

Show me your ways, Lord, teach me your paths.
Guide me in your truth and teach me, for you are
God my Savior, and my hope is in you all day long.
—Psalm 25:4–5 (NIV)

Introduction

For most of my life I've collected words. When I was eight, my mother bought me a sky-blue tablet titled *My First Scribblings.* On its porous pages, I printed words that sounded as pretty on my tongue as they looked on paper. *Enigma. Exquisite. Panacea.*

In elementary school, perplexing tumors began to grow throughout my body. I spent more time in medical waiting rooms than in school classrooms. My disfiguring, painful condition had no name I could scribble in my tablet. I was terrified. But sitting in those waiting rooms, I met some of the bravest—and wisest—people I've ever known. Folks of all ages, from all walks of life. I learned something I've never forgotten. We all struggle. We just struggle in different ways.

I began to notice the most fascinating thing. The patients who spoke certain words—words of hope, faith, and love—seemed to feel better. Live better lives. Somehow make it through those struggles. As time passed, my sky-blue tablet gave way to spiral notebooks as I filled them with the words that I heard. Two decades later, I returned to those pages when choosing a topic for my nursing master's thesis. A young father with what was pronounced to be incurable cancer spoke to me across time. "Hope deferred makes the heart sick," he'd said, reading from the book of Proverbs in the worn black Bible on his lap. Mom and I ran into him throughout his chemo and radiation therapy, after two major surgeries, and finally, when he was pronounced cured.

A single-syllable word had rewritten his story. *Hope.*

That's why the book you hold in your hands means so much to me. Its one hundred days of entries feature a devotional story and a prayer guided by a word that will point you to hope. The authors are much like the patients I met in life's most challenging waiting rooms. Diverse in geographical locations and experiences, their journeys toward hope—toward seeing the good, and true, and beautiful around them—are woven into the fabric of each devotional. You'll find Scriptures for further reflection and a space to record your thoughts.

The stories in this volume remind me of my favorite childhood book, *Charlotte's Web.* Words from its pages are tucked inside a golden frame on my desk: *With the right words, you can change the world.* You really can, you know. The words we speak to ourselves and to others have the power to change your world and mine.

Here's to hope, one of the best words of all. May it be your soul's song.

—Roberta Messner

day 1

welcome

When my son started a lawn business, he got to know one of our neighbors, Mr. B., and they soon became friends. It was an unlikely friendship: Mr. B was a ninety-nine-year-old Jewish Ukrainian immigrant. My son was a Christian Indian-American teenager.

Whenever we visited, he'd welcome us with the kindest, humblest smile. "Thank you for thinking of me," he would say. He was so pleased to have visitors.

Once, he wanted to see a Christmas tree, so we invited him over to see our tree. I made him Indian-style fried rice. He loved it so much, he began making it for his weekly Shabbat dinner. Who would have thought?

We were heartbroken when he passed away at the age of 103. We welcomed him, and he welcomed us, and we were both blessed by this friendship of mutual affection and respect.

—Prasanta Verma

Dear Lord, please help me to welcome others as You have welcomed me. Amen.

Words to Pray On

Welcome one another, therefore, just as Christ has welcomed you, for the glory of God.
—Romans 15:7 (NRSVUE)

Then the king will say to those at his right hand, "Come, you who are blessed by my Father, inherit the kingdom prepared for you from the foundation of the world, for I was hungry and you gave me food, I was thirsty and you gave me something to drink, I was a stranger and you welcomed me."
—Matthew 25:34–35 (NRSVUE)

Whoever welcomes you welcomes me, and whoever welcomes me welcomes the one who sent me.... whoever welcomes a righteous person in the name of a righteous person will receive the reward of the righteous.
—Matthew 10:40–41 (NRSVUE)

_____
_____
_____
_____
_____

day 2

walk

For my grandson's birthday, our family took him to a game facility that included a rope obstacle course that was high in the air. I'm not particularly afraid of heights, so I agreed to harness up and join him on the course.

It all seemed fine—until it wasn't. I did exactly what everyone says not to do—I looked down. Way, way down. I stood frozen to the spot until my grandson looked back and encouraged me. "Come on, Granny! You're hooked onto the rope above you. You can't fall."

I took a deep breath and stepped out, my focus on the clip above me. And I made it to the other side, step by careful step.

I see my walk with God in much the same way. When I hear the still, small voice of God in my heart telling me to walk somewhere new, my first reaction is often to balk. *It's too high up. I'm going to fall.* And yet I hear His gentle word: *Walk.*

The first step is always the hardest.

—Deb Kastner

Lord, help me to walk in the path where You've led me.

Words to Pray On

For we walk by faith, not by sight.
—2 Corinthians 5:7 (NKJV)

Therefore you shall be careful to do as the Lord your God has commanded you; you shall not turn aside to the right hand or to the left. You shall walk in all the ways which the Lord your God has commanded you, that you may live and that it may be well with you, and that you may prolong your days in the land which you shall possess.
—Deuteronomy 5:32–33 (NKJV)

Vindicate me, O Lord, for I have walked in my integrity. I have also trusted in the Lord; I shall not slip. Examine me, O Lord, and prove me; try my mind and my heart. For Your lovingkindness is before my eyes, and I have walked in Your truth.
—Psalm 26:1–3 (NKJV)

day 3

vintage

I've adored vintage objects most of my life. But the way they're described on eBay can sure give one pause. "Condition consistent with age," says a vendor about an old cookie jar. And how's this for a teapot: "spout is cracked but still usable." Or the handmade vintage quilt: "A little worse for wear but great as a decorative accent."

Chalk it up to my old-school mentality, but those words used to remind me of myself. Until four years ago, that is, when a miracle of God took away a lifetime of agony. Folks had to remind me what my pain was like; I didn't even recognize my new body.

Recently I found a wonderful new doctor who is board-certified in both internal medicine and pediatrics. Wouldn't you agree it's a match made in heaven? I'm not vintage. At four years new, I'm a certified toddler.

—Roberta Messner

Vintage doesn't exist in Your vocabulary, Lord. When we entrust our lives to You, we are new every morning.

Words to Pray On

Therefore, if anyone is in Christ, the new creation has come: The old has gone, the new is here!

—2 Corinthians 5:17 (NIV)

Sing to the Lord a new song, for he has done marvelous things; his right hand and his holy arm have worked salvation for him.

—Psalm 98:1 (NIV)

See, I will create new heavens and a new earth. The former things will not be remembered, nor will they come to mind. But be glad and rejoice forever in what I will create, for I will create Jerusalem to be a delight and its people a joy.

—Isaiah 65:17–18 (NIV)

day 4

notice

I flew alone for the first time when my husband graduated from Officer Indoctrination School in Rhode Island as a Navy entomologist. The flight marked only the second occasion I'd taken to the air—the first was my honeymoon. A distinguished-looking, grandfatherly gentleman noticed my apprehension as we disembarked and pointed me to baggage claim. When I told him I'd traveled north to see my husband graduate from OIS, he recommended the proper shuttle for my destination.

Imagine my surprise when I saw that same gentleman, Commodore Caudill, address the Navy graduates at the ceremony. My husband, David, showed even greater surprise when the two of us made our way through the receiving line and Commodore Caudill called me by name. Out of earshot, David whispered, "How do you know the keynote speaker?" I just smiled and said, "Oh, he noticed this frightened little Southern girl on an airplane and extended kindness."
—Julie Lavender

Thank You, God, that You notice me and I find favor with You, for that is quite a treasure. Help me notice others, too, especially in their time of need. Amen.

Words to Pray On

At this, she bowed down with her face to the ground. She asked him, "Why have I found such favor in your eyes that you notice me—a foreigner?"

—Ruth 2:10 (NIV)

She gave this name to the Lord who spoke to her: "You are the God who sees me," for she said, "I have now seen the One who sees me."

—Genesis 16:13 (NIV)

O Lord, what are human beings that you should notice them, mere mortals that you should think about them? For they are like a breath of air; their days are like a passing shadow.

—Psalm 144:3–4 (NLT)

day 5

enlightened

You don't realize what you can't see until you can see—until your eyes become enlightened. I recently had cataracts removed after waiting for several years for them to "ripen." When I opened my eyes after surgery, my worldview quickly and unexpectedly became illuminated. Objects were free of darkness, cloudiness was gone, opaque became transparent, and everything of substance was impregnated with color. My enlightened vision empowered my mind to take in new perceptions about my world. What I once viewed as truth shifted. Life transformed with the light.

We are spiritually enlightened when we read God's word. God's word is a lamp that lights our path and secures our walk. It removes the spiritual cataracts that distort our perceptions and views. Enlightened eyes clearly see. Distortion, confusion, and hazy vision become clear, sharp, and focused.

—Betty A. Rodgers-Kulich

Jesus, shine in my darkness and upon my faith walk. Remove any spiritual cataracts so I can see clearly what the darkness has distorted and reveal what I have grown accustomed to. Amen.

Words to Pray On

That the God of our Lord Jesus Christ, the Father of glory, may give to you the spirit of wisdom and revelation in the knowledge of Him, the eyes of your understanding being enlightened; that you may know what is the hope of His calling....

—Ephesians 1:17–18 (NKJV)

For You are my lamp, O Lord; the Lord shall enlighten my darkness. For by You I can run against a troop; by my God I can leap over a wall.

—2 Samuel 22:29–30 (NKJV)

The commandment of the Lord is pure, enlightening the eyes; the fear of the Lord is clean, enduring forever; the judgments of the Lord are true and righteous altogether.

—Psalm 19:8–9 (NKJV)

day 6

beauty

"I have to tell you, you're beautiful. Your smile, your hair—it's all working today," I told the flight attendant as I boarded the plane. Her smile widened a little. Thinking back on it, I'm not sure she looked convinced.

I settled in under my noise-canceling headphones, slept for most of the flight, and woke up to sneak a quick drink order in under the wire from that same flight attendant. She delivered it with two napkins—one for my use, and one covered with a personal note scratched out in pen:

"My boyfriend broke up with me in a text last week. I've been so sad, and I've been feeling so ugly and insecure. I needed you today. Thank you for your love and your light. It meant the world to me."

All I did was tell her she was beautiful.

Who might need to hear this from you today?

—Laurie Davies

Lord, give us eyes to see the things You don't want us to miss. Amen.

Words to Pray On

He has made everything beautiful in its time. He has also set eternity in the human heart; yet no one can fathom what God has done from beginning to end.
—Ecclesiastes 3:11 (NIV)

A person finds joy in giving an apt reply—and how good is a timely word!
—Proverbs 15:23 (NIV)

Do not let any unwholesome talk come out of your mouths, but only what is helpful for building others up according to their needs, that it may benefit those who listen.
—Ephesians 4:29 (NIV)

day 7

enthusiasm

When we plan a vacation, a birthday, a date night, or a visit from our best friend, we often meet the day with enthusiasm. Imagine if we met each day with that special feeling of delight and expectation, thinking about what God has in store for us? What if we woke up with the hope of an adventure—one that God is in control of—in our heart? Each day we are presented with opportunities and unexpected delights if only we look for the presence of God in our life.

Slow down, look at the moments, and notice the good about each day. Pray the word *enthusiasm* today and meet your prayer and worship time with the possibility of unexpected gifts.

—Rebecca Chamaa

Dear God, please fill me with enthusiasm for the unexpected gifts and answered prayer You bring to my life.

Words to Pray On

For I know your eagerness to help, and I have been boasting about it to the Macedonians, telling them that since last year you in Achaia were ready to give; and your enthusiasm has stirred most of them to action.
—2 Corinthians 9:2 (NIV)

They sought God eagerly, and he was found by them. So the Lord gave them rest on every side.
—2 Chronicles 15:15 (NIV)

Now finish the work, so that your eager willingness to do it may be matched by your completion of it, according to your means.
—2 Corinthians 8:11 (NIV)

day 8

possible

Gizmo, our Lhasa Apso, was gone. Our German shepherd, aptly named Licky, had dug a hole beneath our fence, and Gizmo had followed him through it. But Licky returned alone.

We lived on a busy street where few drivers obeyed the speed limit. And to make matters worse, Gizmo was as black as the night sky.

I searched for hours, shouting his name until I was exhausted and hoarse. I gave up and called my best friend.

"It feels hopeless. I'm afraid that he's been hit by a car or lost."

"It isn't hopeless. All things are possible with God. Let's pray," Carol said.

That night I repeated, "All things are possible with God," before falling into a fitful sleep. I was wakened by a cold wet tongue licking my chin.

"Go away, Licky. It's your fault," I grumbled, then realized that it was Gizmo licking my face. He was home!

—Kristy Dewberry

Heavenly Father, today I pray and choose to believe that what seems impossible is possible if I trust in You.

Words to Pray On

Everything is possible for one who believes.
—Mark 9:23 (NIV)

When he had gone indoors, the blind men came to him, and he asked them, "Do you believe that I am able to do this?" "Yes, Lord," they replied. Then he touched their eyes and said, "According to your faith let it be done to you"; and their sight was restored.
—Matthew 9:28–30 (NIV)

Praise be to the name of God for ever and ever; wisdom and power are his. He changes times and seasons; he deposes kings and raises up others. He gives wisdom to the wise and knowledge to the discerning. He reveals deep and hidden things; he knows what lies in darkness, and light dwells with him.
—Daniel 2:20–22 (NIV)

day 9

daffodils

One spring, my brother and I were near some woods on his property. An area about the size of a basketball court was filled with yellow daffodils. He said it was the site of an old homestead. The original structure was long gone, but some early settler must have had hope in a new beginning and in a spring that would bring daffodils. And then the flowers carried on when no one was around to watch. That long-forgotten act of planting is still giving beauty many lifetimes later.

I wonder how many of our acts will outlive us. I'm remembering now so many people who had positive effects on my life and enabled me to achieve what I wanted to do. Many of them—like this early settler—are no longer around for me to thank.

I find it fitting that daffodils are known for symbolizing rebirth, new beginnings, and love. Like this pioneer's plantings, may my life's work be plantings for the future.

—Nancy Schrock

Lord, I have hope that the fruits of our labors continue to sprout for generations, like daffodils in the spring.

Words to Pray On

Remember me with favor, my God.
—Nehemiah 13:31 (NIV)

See! The winter is past; the rains are over and gone. Flowers appear on the earth; the season of singing has come, the cooing of doves is heard in our land.
—Song of Songs 2:11–12 (NIV)

For as the soil makes the sprout come up and a garden causes seed to grow, so the Sovereign Lord will make righteousness and praise spring up before all the nations.
—Isaiah 61:11 (NIV)

Truly I tell you, wherever the gospel is preached throughout the world, what she has done will also be told, in memory of her.
—Mark 14:9 (NIV)

_____
_____
_____
_____
_____

day 10

lament

Recently, an email with the subject line Lamentations 3:22 arrived in my morning inbox. It's a verse I know by heart.

Eight years ago, when my stepson Ryan was killed in a tragic accident, that verse played a starring role in my journal. Those first few months after Ry's death, I hung out in the pages of Lamentations reading verses 3:19–26 while lamenting to God about how much I was hurting. The emotional weight of those words would cause tears to fall on the opaque pages of my Bible.

The days turned into months. Even when I couldn't feel myself turning the corner on grief, I found that the more I cried out to God, the stronger my faith became.

Those words are now a mantra of the truth that God hears my pain, and I can trust Him to walk me through it.

—Amy Catlin Wozniak

Dear Lord, help us to cry out to You in lament, knowing You will walk us through the trials we face in this fallen world. Amen.

Words to Pray On

I remember my affliction and my wandering, the bitterness and the gall. I well remember them, and my soul is downcast within me. Yet this I call to mind and therefore I have hope: Because of the Lord's great love we are not consumed, for his compassions never fail. They are new every morning; great is your faithfulness. I say to myself, "The Lord is my portion; therefore I will wait for him." The Lord is good to those whose hope is in him; to the one who seeks him; it is good to wait quietly for the salvation of the Lord.

—Lamentations 3:19–26 (NIV)

day 11

spacious

One of the longest floating bridges in the world connects our peninsula with the mainland. Spanning a distance of nearly one-and-a-half miles, the Hood Canal Bridge welcomes travelers to a wide and spacious panorama of mountains and sea. Each time I arrive at the bend in the road that leads to the bridge and that spectacular view, I pause and take a deep breath. My heart expands with joy.

After the Israelites' long, forty-year journey in the wilderness—described in the text of Psalm 66 on the opposite page—they arrived at the Jordan River. God had delivered them from servitude in Egypt and from the perils of the desert. Now their spacious new home lay before them. Their hearts overflowed in gratitude for the gift of God's salvation.

—Marlene Kropf

Liberating God, You set us free from sin and death; You bring us out to the spaciousness of life with You. Amen.

Words to Pray On

Bless our God, O peoples; let the sound of his praise be heard, who has kept us among the living and has not let our feet slip. For you, O God, have tested us; you have tried us as silver is tried. You brought us into the net; you laid burdens on our backs; you let people ride over our heads; we went through fire and through water; yet you have brought us out to a spacious place.

—Psalm 66:8–12 (NRSVUE)

Indeed, I know their sufferings, and I have come down to deliver them from the Egyptians and to bring them up out of that land to a good and spacious land, to a land flowing with milk and honey…

—Exodus 3:7–8 (NRSVUE)

day 12

magnify

I will never forget the time when we gave our six-year-old grandson a magnifying glass with a light. He carried it around for a long time, looking at the enlargement of many objects under the light of his new instrument.

We don't need a magnifying glass when it comes to God. He is everywhere. In fact, Paul tells us in Romans that even God's invisible attributes are clearly seen in creation, so that no one has an excuse not to believe in Him.

The fullness of God's divine presence in our daily lives gives us true reason to bow down and worship Him. He is able to do abundantly more than we can ask or imagine, and His spirit fills every place in creation.

Our God is big. We can always find Him.
—Becky Van Vleet

O Lord, we magnify You for who You are, for what You're doing, and for what You're going to do in each of our lives.

Words to Pray On

Oh, magnify the Lord with me, and let us exalt His name together.
—Psalm 34:3 (NKJV)

For since the creation of the world His invisible attributes are clearly seen, being understood by the things that are made, even His eternal power and Godhead, so that they are without excuse, because, although they knew God, they did not glorify Him as God, nor were thankful, but became futile in their thoughts, and their foolish hearts were darkened.
—Romans 1:20–21 (NKJV)

Remember to magnify His work, of which men have sung. Everyone has seen it; man looks on it from afar.
—Job 36:24–25 (NKJV)

_____
_____
_____
_____
_____

day 13

builder

My pastor shared a dream he had that helped me to understand the depth of God's involvement in my life. In the dream, Jesus was moving intentionally around a brickyard, dressed in dusty overalls and work boots. The yard was littered with bricks, some heaped in piles, some loose stragglers off by themselves, none appearing to have any pattern to their placement.

As Jesus worked, lifting one brick at a time, He knew what He was doing. He had a plan that directed His movements. Some bricks were transferred a great distance from where they had lain, while others were nudged just a bit to bring them into the alignment He wanted for them. And while the work looked tedious and tiring, Jesus had a smile on His face the entire time.

—Liz Kimmel

Teach me to rest in Your plan for my life. Amen.

Words to Pray On

For every house is built by someone, but God is the builder of everything.

—Hebrews 3:4 (NIV)

And it will be said: "Build up, build up, prepare the road! Remove the obstacles out of the way of my people."

—Isaiah 57:14 (NIV)

Unless the Lord builds the house, the builders labor in vain. Unless the Lord watches over the city, the guards stand watch in vain. In vain you rise early and stay up late, toiling for food to eat—for he grants sleep to those he loves.

—Psalm 127:1–2 (NIV)

day 14

family

It started out as an ordinary December day. I shopped all day for Christmas gifts. I had a late lunch with my husband, and that evening we headed to our Wednesday-night church service. I felt unusually energetic. Our church's six garbage cans lined the highway, so my husband and I pulled them to their rightful place outside our kitchen/fellowship area.

Suddenly, my energy dissipated, and I was overcome with weakness. I faded to black, feeling life leave my body. I awoke on the pavement with my church family and my husband begging God for my life.

On January 8, I underwent open heart surgery. My pastor came to the operating room and prayed for me. My praying church family called every day, sent cards, and after I recovered, they welcomed my return.

Thank God for my family of believers. They offer love, encouragement, and fellowship, and they make me feel secure because I know that God is in the midst of them.

—Jessica Roach Ferguson

Dear Heavenly Father, I thank You for a church family that can pray for each other with the power of Your love.

Words to Pray On

Again, truly I tell you that if two of you on earth agree about anything they ask for, it will be done for them by my Father in heaven. For where two or three gather in my name, there am I with them.
—Matthew 18:19–20 (NIV)

Both the one who makes people holy and those who are made holy are of the same family. So Jesus is not ashamed to call them brothers and sisters. He says, "I will declare your name to my brothers and sisters; in the assembly I will sing your praises." And again, "I will put my trust in him." And again he says, "Here am I, and the children God has given me."
—Hebrews 2:11–13 (NIV)

What gives me the most hope every day is God's grace; knowing that His grace is going to give me the strength for whatever I face, knowing that nothing is a surprise to God.
—Rick Warren

day 15

seal

Led by therapists and people of faith, the retreat's focus was "forgiveness."

"Now, pick blindly from this bag," the therapist instructed, "a stuffed animal, a symbol of your work on forgiveness. Share the first words that come to mind."

I picked a seal. Ugh! Awkward animals, ugly sounds. Words? Blank.

Holy Spirit, help! I prayed.

The words came. "I am sealed with God's love."

I forgave my parents. Deeply. Every nook and cranny of my heart. With forgiveness came compassion. They survived their own wretched childhoods. Love sealed my heart.

My father had died. From the stars he winks at me nightly.

From Mom, silent anger. Love persistently guided me. Finally, peace. Six months later, I was privileged to care for Mom as she lay dying.

The stuffed seal? A reminder: forgiveness, a daily task where miracles abound.

"Sealed with my love." Not my words. God's.

—Mayra Fernandez

Father, help me forgive more deeply every day.

Words to Pray On

Set me as a seal upon your heart, as a seal upon your arm; for love is as strong as death.
—Song of Solomon 8:6 (NKJV)

For God may speak in one way, or in another, yet man does not perceive it. In a dream, in a vision of the night, when deep sleep falls upon men, while slumbering on their beds, then He opens the ears of men, and seals their instruction.
—Job 33:14–16 (NKJV)

Do not labor for food which perishes, but for the food which endures to everlasting life, which the Son of Man will give you, because God the Father has set His seal on Him.
—John 6:27 (NKJV)

day 16

flourish

The year I turned fifty, we celebrated with a family vacation to the beach. Early one morning, I packed up a folding chair, a travel mug of coffee (with plenty of creamer), and my Bible and notebook, setting off for some alone time with Jesus.

Even amidst the beauty of the towering palm trees; the cool, sparkling water; and the steady lapping waves on the sand, I found myself lamenting this new season of life. I felt old and dried up.

I scanned the Scriptures, praying for a word from the Lord. My eyes were drawn to the words of Psalm 92: "The righteous will flourish like a palm tree.... They will bear fruit in old age. They will stay fresh and green...."

My heart rejoiced in this reassurance from the Lord. In Christ, I will stay fresh and green. No matter what age I reach, I can flourish and bear fruit!

—Mindy Baker

Lord, I pray that I may flourish like a palm tree, bearing fruit for Your Kingdom. Amen.

Words to Pray On

The righteous will flourish like a palm tree, they will grow like a cedar of Lebanon; planted in the house of the Lord, they will flourish in the courts of our God. They will still bear fruit in old age, they will stay fresh and green, proclaiming, "The Lord is upright; he is my Rock, and there is no wickedness in him."
—Psalm 92:12–15 (NIV)

But I am like an olive tree flourishing in the house of God; I trust in God's unfailing love for ever and ever. For what you have done I will always praise you in the presence of your faithful people. And I will hope in your name, for your name is good.
—Psalm 52:8–9 (NIV)

day 17

sees

In Genesis 16, when the servant Hagar is treated harshly by her mistress, Sarai, she runs away and wanders through the desert.

While I have never been lost in a literal desert, I have found myself in a spiritual wilderness more than once. While not an easy journey to take, during these challenging times in life—without fail—God has been with me, offering the reassurance that He sees me. Whether I am sick, stressed, or insecure, He sees me.

This word *sees* is a powerful word describing a specific action that God takes with His creation. He sees us because He chooses to, and the word *sees* is one we can reflect back to Him in prayer. When in doubt or when feeling unworthy, we can be sure that God sees us.

—Laurel Shaler

Dear Lord, thank You for being the God who sees us. Amen.

Words to Pray On

Thereafter, Hagar used another name to refer to the Lord, who had spoken to her. She said, "You are the God who sees me." She also said, "Have I truly seen the One who sees me?"

—Genesis 16:13 (NLT)

Solomon, my son, learn to know the God of your ancestors intimately. Worship and serve him with your whole heart and a willing mind. For the Lord sees every heart and knows every plan and thought. If you seek him, you will find him.

—1 Chronicles 28:9 (NLT)

God alone understands the way to wisdom; he knows where it can be found, for he looks throughout the whole earth, and sees everything under the heavens.

—Job 28:23–24 (NLT)

day 18

pleasure

"When I run, I feel His pleasure," sprinter Eric Liddell told his sister, trying to explain why he was training for the Olympics and delaying his start on the mission field. He went on to win two medals in the 1924 Olympics, including a gold in the 400-meter race.

I have thought of this quote many times, especially during the long and weary days of the pandemic. I kept a small notebook by my bed and listed moments of pleasure from the day. A flock of robins on the front lawn pecking for worms after a rain. Pleasure. The softness of my granddaughter's hand in mine. Pleasure. The yapping joy of dogs wrestling and chasing at the dog park. Pleasure. The kaleidoscope of colors in a bowl of summer fruit. Pleasure.

Recording these flashes of pleasure made me more attentive to other moments that I might otherwise have overlooked. They also connected me to the Creator of these pleasures, and reminded me that His gifts, like His mercies, are abundant and new every day.

—Mary Hix

Loving Creator, help me to notice and feel Your pleasure in the moments of this day. Amen.

Words to Pray On

They shall praise His name with dancing; they shall sing praises to Him with tambourine and lyre. For the LORD takes pleasure in His people; He will glorify the lowly with salvation. The godly ones shall be jubilant in glory; they shall sing for joy on their beds.
—Psalm 149:3–5 (NASB)

I know, my God, that you search the heart and take pleasure in uprightness; in the uprightness of my heart I have freely offered all these things, and now I have seen your people who are present here offering freely and joyously to you.
—1 Chronicles 29:17 (NRSVUE)

You show me the path of life. In your presence there is fullness of joy; in your right hand are pleasures forevermore.
—Psalm 16:11 (NRSVUE)

day 19

accomplishment

My almost eight-year-old son ran into my office holding a sheet of paper and beaming with pride. "Look Momma," he said, "I drew a person!"

As I peeked at the page, sure enough, there was a person-like figure on it with all the features you would expect, and not just a stick figure. He was so happy because he knew most of his peers had reached this milestone a couple of years ago. Drawing and coloring were never skills he showed interest or proficiency in during kindergarten or first grade, so this was a big accomplishment for him.

As I watched my copy paper supply dwindle over the next few weeks as he honed his new skills, I could only smile and thank God for my son's accomplishment.
—Donna Pryor

Lord, let us always remember to celebrate our accomplishments and the accomplishments of others, no matter the size. Amen.

Words to Pray On

A desire accomplished is sweet to the soul...
—Proverbs 13:19 (NKJV)

So shall My word be that goes forth from My mouth; it shall not return to Me void, but it shall accomplish what I please, and it shall prosper in the thing for which I sent it.
—Isaiah 55:11 (NKJV)

Lord, you establish peace for us; all that we have accomplished you have done for us.
—Isaiah 26:12 (NIV)

And Moses said to the people, "Do not be afraid. Stand still, and see the salvation of the Lord, which He will accomplish for you today."
—Exodus 14:13 (NKJV)

day 20

edit

In the week after my father's death, the apartment had been emptied down to only a few lingering treasures. An easy chair where he used to sit. A couple of dress shirts he wore on special occasions. A box of books—Whitman, Poe, and others—with his craggy signature inside. Now they belonged to me. After seventy-seven years of love, war, marriage, career, kids, grandkids, and the loss of his wife, my dad had lived his life well, his story masterfully edited. Unlike mine.

Between the stress of jobs, the demands of social media, and other time-stealers that wreak havoc on the years, I pray that God will take a big red pen and start editing the parts of my life that lead me away from Him. Correct my future mistakes, replace the careless words on my tongue, and amend my wayward direction. Revise my life to serve God's story well and to honor its Managing Editor.

—Kimberly Shumate

To You, Lord, the author and editor of history, guide my character to live a life that reflects Your perfect Word. Amen.

Words to Pray On

...all the days ordained for me were written in your book before one of them came to be.

—Psalm 139:16 (NIV)

Let the redeemed of the Lord tell their story—those he redeemed from the hand of the foe, those he gathered from the lands, from east and west, from north and south.

—Psalm 107:2–3 (NIV)

The tablets were the work of God; the writing was the writing of God, engraved on the tablets.

—Exodus 32:16 (NIV)

"All this," David said, "I have in writing as a result of the Lord's hand on me, and he enabled me to understand all the details of the plan."

—1 Chronicles 28:19 (NIV)

_____
_____
_____
_____

day 21

desire

Desire. We all experience it. By definition, desire means a strong feeling, a deep intention or aim. It's often visualized as warmth, heat, or burning fire. We experience a strong attraction or "pull" toward the person or thing we desire, and our actions spring from our desires.

Desire is a common human emotion. But I had a revelation when I realized that *God* has strong desires, and that He desires *me*. Broken, crusty old me, with all my warts on full display. Because of this desire, God made a way for me to come back to Him. His actions sprang from His own desire, sending Jesus to die in my place, so I might be restored to Him. It revolutionized my life and gave me the courage to follow Him.

—Renee Yancy

Lord, thank You for the amazing gift of Your desire.

Words to Pray On

I am my beloved's, and his desire is for me.
—Song of Solomon 7:10 (NASB)

Lord, all my desire is before You; and my sighing is not hidden from You.... For I wait for You, Lord; You will answer, Lord my God.
—Psalm 38:9, 15 (NASB)

Indeed, while following the way of Your judgments, Lord, we have waited for You eagerly; Your name, and remembering You, is the desire of our souls.
—Isaiah 26:8 (NASB)

Those who live according to the flesh have their minds set on what the flesh desires; but those who live in accordance with the Spirit have their minds set on what the Spirit desires.
—Romans 8:5 (NIV)

day 22

mess

She covered her face as the shame reddened her cheeks. "I'm so embarrassed." My friend had a long-term illness and her house was in disrepair. She finally let me in to help her, but the mess was deep. As I began to clean a particularly dirty corner, I glanced over to see the tears in her eyes. I went to her and hugged her close. "Thank you for letting me in and trusting me today. I'm so happy to help you."

As I turned back to the mess, I could barely hold back my own tears. *This is just what God does.* He sees the mess. He loves us still. He must be so proud when we let Him in. When we trust Him with our stuff. When we lean into His goodness in the midst of the chaos.

—Elsa Kok Colopy

Thank You, Lord, for coming into my mess. Without condemnation, You survey it all and help me, one dusty corner at a time.

Words to Pray On

You see, at just the right time, when we were still powerless, Christ died for the ungodly. Very rarely will anyone die for a righteous person, though for a good person someone might possibly dare to die. But God demonstrates his own love for us in this: While we were still sinners, Christ died for us.

—Romans 5:6–8 (NIV)

The righteous cry out, and the Lord hears them; he delivers them from all their troubles. The Lord is close to the brokenhearted and saves those who are crushed in spirit. The righteous person may have many troubles, but the Lord delivers him from them all; he protects all his bones, not one of them will be broken.

—Psalm 34:17–20 (NIV)

day 23

letters

I have a letter-a-day habit. What started as a discipline during Lent years ago has become a ministry. I write to widows. I remember birthdays. I cheer on kiddos. I encourage chemo patients. I send mail to online friends. Anyone and everyone in my life is on my mailing list. I send love through the postal service.

Sending a letter is a gentle way to connect. It is more personal than a text, more lasting than a phone call, and unexpected in our technology-filled world. A letter takes time to create and can sit on a loved one's table long after it's been received. Letters are a unique way to carry each other's burdens and share each other's joys.

—Lisa Bogart

Father, call to mind someone in my life who needs to hear from me. Someone I can show my love with a handwritten letter. Amen.

Words to Pray On

Help carry each other's burdens. In this way you will follow Christ's teachings.
—Galatians 6:2 (GW)

We encourage you, brothers and sisters, to... cheer up those who are discouraged, help the weak, and be patient with everyone. Make sure that no one ever pays back one wrong with another wrong. Instead, always try to do what is good for each other and everyone else.
—1 Thessalonians 5:14–15 (GW)

God in his kindness gave each of us different gifts. If your gift is speaking what God has revealed, make sure what you say agrees with the Christian faith. If your gift is serving, then devote yourself to serving. If it is teaching, devote yourself to teaching. If it is encouraging others, devote yourself to giving encouragement.
—Romans 12:6–8 (GW)

day 24

cast

I knew immediately I'd made a faux pas. I'd said the wrong thing to a powerful person in my field. Maybe even offended her. Her correction was gracious. I thanked her. And the moment was over. But it was not over in my mind.

Repeatedly, I replayed the conversation, cringing as I imagined her distaste. Anxiety twisted my gut. I wanted to apologize. To explain myself. But that would only make it worse. She'd already moved on.

I decided to obey God and cast my anxiety on Him. "I cast my anxiety and this whole situation on You, Lord," I prayed. "I trust You to care for me."

Anytime the memory returned, I released it to God again.

A year later, that same lady surprised me by giving me the sweetest, heartfelt compliment. I'm so glad I cast my anxiety on Jesus.

Anxiety never helps. It's much better to cast.

—Jenny Snow

Lord, I cast any anxiety I've been carrying onto You. I know that You care for me, and I trust my life completely to You. Amen.

Words to Pray On

Cast all your anxiety on him because he cares for you.
—1 Peter 5:7 (NIV)

Cast your cares on the Lord and he will sustain you; he will never let the righteous be shaken.
—Psalm 55:22 (NIV)

When I said, "My foot is slipping," your unfailing love, Lord, supported me. When anxiety was great within me, your consolation brought me joy.
—Psalm 94:18–19 (NIV)

Anxiety weighs down the heart, but a kind word cheers it up.
—Proverbs 12:25 (NIV)

day 25

perspective

We took a quick getaway to a resort up north. To my dismay, the word *resort* no longer applied. The motel was tired and run down. Seeing my disappointment, my husband quickly herded us out of our dingy room to climb the hundred-year-old watchtower.

As the wood creaked beneath our feet, I envisioned it crumbling and taking us down with it. At the top, I looked up for the first time. My breath was taken away! The view of the White Mountains was spectacular, the changing leaves painting the view with blazing yellows, oranges, and reds. Our dreary motel was just a speck amidst the brilliance of God's paintbrush.

Perspective is everything. When I look down and criticize all that's not right, I miss the wondrous things God is doing above my sightline. It takes raising my eyes to see His hand at work, creating beaty and grace everywhere.

—Claire McGarry

Creator of Brilliance, prompt me to lift my eyes above what I see and trust You are working for my good. Amen.

Words to Pray On

So we fix our eyes not on what is seen, but on what is unseen, since what is seen is temporary, but what is unseen is eternal.
—2 Corinthians 4:18 (NIV)

The Lord looked down from his sanctuary on high, from heaven he viewed the earth...
—Psalm 102:19 (NIV)

A discerning person keeps wisdom in view, but a fool's eyes wander to the ends of the earth.
—Proverbs 17:24 (NIV)

So from now on we regard no one from a worldly point of view.
—2 Corinthians 5:16 (NIV)

day 26

found

We'd been together constantly from the start. For two years, we ventured into stores, restaurants, clinics, and gatherings. We even took trips together. I loved my homemade mask, a gift from my neighbor Marcella. Its cartoony monkey features always made me smile.

Then one day I couldn't find my monkey mask. I searched everywhere. I asked at the pantry where I volunteer. But no luck. I'd lost my mask. I felt ridiculous for missing it.

Soon my pantry shift came around again. I stepped into the food storage room and gasped. Someone had found my monkey mask and hung it on a shelf! I whooped with joy. Though worthless and replaceable, the mask was special. Given with love and worn with joy, it felt like a dear friend had been returned to me.

—Sheryl Smith-Rodgers

Lord, even a silly lost mask, when found, matters to You. Nothing is too small for You.

Words to Pray On

Or suppose a woman has ten silver coins and loses one. Doesn't she light a lamp, sweep the house and search carefully until she finds it? And when she finds it, she calls her friends and neighbors together and says, "Rejoice with me; I have found my lost coin."

—Luke 15:8–9 (NIV)

So I came out to meet you; I looked for you and have found you!

—Proverbs 7:15 (NIV)

And Isaiah boldly says, "I was found by those who did not seek me; I revealed myself to those who did not ask for me."

—Romans 10:20 (NIV)

day 27

doubt

When I first contacted Felicia, then seven years into her ten-year prison sentence, her doubt that God would accept her was fierce. Felicia is the daughter of my younger sister Colleen. I had never met Felicia, but knew about her from my phone calls with Colleen about her family life.

I set up conversations with Felicia after seeking God's message on how I could do more to advance His kingdom. "Start with the family I've given you," He said. It was a leap of faith over my own mountain of doubt.

Felicia had done some stupendously bad things. Her shame poured gasoline on the burning pile of doubt that she could be "saved." I shared many of my shortcomings and past doubt about God's grace.

With time, Felicia was transformed. A felon's doubt turned into a bold belief. My waffling doubt in God's endless love took another kick in the pants.

—Kenneth Avon White

Father, help me never doubt how deep is Your love and wide Your grace.

Words to Pray On

For I will be merciful to their unrighteousness, and their sins and their lawless deeds I will remember no more.
—Hebrews 8:12 (NKJV)

I said, "Lord, be merciful to me; heal my soul, for I have sinned against You."

—Psalm 41:4 (NKJV)

If any of you lacks wisdom, let him ask of God, who gives to all liberally and without reproach, and it will be given to him. But let him ask in faith, with no doubting, for he who doubts is like a wave of the sea driven and tossed by the wind.

—James 1:5–6 (NKJV)

day 28

hold

We are halfway through a one-thousand-mile road trip when we hit black ice.

"Everyone, hold on," my husband says. A quick, panicked survey of the scene shows three cars already in the median and one flipped on its side. A semi-trailer truck slithers like a mechanical snake in and out of our lane. Everything is moving, and we're at the mercy of momentum.

What can I hold on to? I hear my voice cry in prayer, "Oh Lord, please..." thinking of our children in the back seat. My husband steadies the SUV as best he can, then drives directly onto the median at sixty miles per hour. We plunge into thick snow, and he keeps moving until we're a safe distance from the crash site. I reach back and hold our kids' hands and calm my racing heart.

In a terrifying burst of moments when everything felt out of control, I held onto what is steady—a God who is always holding me.

— Eryn Lynum

Dear Lord, when everything feels out of control, I hold on to Your steadfast hope, and I will not be shaken. Amen.

Words to Pray On

For I am the Lord your God who takes hold of your right hand and says to you, Do not fear; I will help you.
—Isaiah 41:13 (NIV)

I cling to you; your right hand upholds me.
—Psalm 63:8 (NIV)

Yet I am always with you; you hold me by my right hand. You guide me with your counsel, and afterward you will take me into glory. Whom have I in heaven but you? And earth has nothing I desire besides you. My flesh and my heart may fail, but God is the strength of my heart and my portion forever.
—Psalm 73:23–26 (NIV)

One must not despair of God,
for hope is the first step on the
road to salvation. Even if you do
not travel the road, at least keep
the road open.
—Rumi

day 29

risk

For years, I was fearful of rejection, abandonment, and the pain of disappointment. So I wove an emotional cocoon, refusing to expose my heart to the risk of being laughed at, left out, or left behind. But Jesus beckoned me to step out, Lazarus-like, from the graveclothes of my own weaving.

C.S. Lewis understood this struggle. In his book *The Lion, the Witch and the Wardrobe*, Mr. Beaver refers to Aslan (a Jesus figure) by saying, "Safe?... Who said anything about safe? 'Course he isn't safe. But he's good."

Jesus invites us into the adventure of trusting Him. Will we risk rejection and hurt? Yes. But will He safeguard our souls? Absolutely.

I've chosen to trust the Lord to protect and bless me as I unfold my wings, shed my cocoon, and fly with Him.

—Leslie McLeod

Jesus, I'm so grateful that You understand my fears but offer me joy as I cast them aside to follow You.

Words to Pray On

The name of the Lord is a fortified tower; the righteous run to it and are safe.

—Proverbs 18:10 (NIV)

But you will cross the Jordan and settle in the land the Lord your God is giving you as an inheritance, and he will give you rest from all your enemies around you so that you will live in safety.

—Deuteronomy 12:10 (NIV)

After this, the word of the Lord came to Abram in a vision: "Do not be afraid, Abram. I am your shield, your very great reward...." He also said to him, "I am the Lord, who brought you out of Ur of the Chaldeans to give you this land to take possession of it."

—Genesis 15:1, 7 (NIV)

day 30

childlike

As soon as my godson appeared in the sunlit doorway, I noticed a change.

The toddler with curly brown hair no longer saw me as a stranger. Gone were the questioning eyes trying to place who I was. No, this time his face flooded with recognition. He opened his arms wide, rushing to embrace me with wobbly legs that were still learning how to walk.

My godson wasn't focused on pride or possessions. He wasn't distracted by resentment or jealousy. His heart was pure, trusting. His motive was *love*—ready to give it and eager to receive it.

In many ways, children are models of faith. Let's approach Jesus with childlike trust today—with abundant love and pure hearts. His loving arms will guide our own "wobbly legs" through every step of life.

—Lauren Craft

Father, I am Your child. I open my heart to Your love and guidance today. Amen.

Words to Pray On

Then people brought little children to Jesus for him to place his hands on them and pray for them. But the disciples rebuked them. Jesus said, "Let the little children come to me, and do not hinder them, for the kingdom of heaven belongs to such as these."
—Matthew 19:13–14 (NIV)

At that time the disciples came to Jesus and asked, "Who, then, is the greatest in the kingdom of heaven?" He called a little child to him, and placed the child among them. And he said: "Truly I tell you, unless you change and become like little children, you will never enter the kingdom of heaven. Therefore, whoever takes the lowly position of this child is the greatest in the kingdom of heaven. And whoever welcomes one such child in my name welcomes me."
—Matthew 18:1–5 (NIV)

day 31

thrive

I decided to treat myself to a half-day retreat at a local arboretum, complete with a yoga class, to celebrate surviving two years of pandemic living. My husband—knowing how I'd schooled our children at home, grocery-shopped for a full week at a time while wearing gloves, and missed fellowship at church—said, "You survived!" I appreciated his efforts to praise me, but moments later I thought, *But I want to thrive.*

I believe God wants us all to thrive. I spent part of my retreat taking stock of my current circumstances, and then jotted some notes about how I wanted to thrive in my own life. At the top of the list was feeling physically healthy, because I knew a sense of well-being would spill over into my entire life. I set some exercise goals and added an entry to my prayer list: *Show me, Lord, how You see me thriving.* I know that when the time is right, He will lead me to the next step.

—Becky Hofstad

Lord, please help me identify the steps I need to take to blossom and thrive. Amen.

Words to Pray On

As you lay there, I said, "Live!" And I helped you to thrive like a plant in the field. You grew up and became a beautiful jewel.

—Ezekiel 16:6–7 (NLT)

May there be abundant grain throughout the land, flourishing even on the hilltops. May the fruit trees flourish like the trees of Lebanon, and may the people thrive like grass in a field.

—Psalm 72:16 (NLT)

For I will pour out water to quench your thirst and to irrigate your parched fields. And I will pour out my Spirit on your descendants, and my blessing on your children. They will thrive like watered grass, like willows on a riverbank.

—Isaiah 44:3–4 (NLT)

day 32

wonder

Sometimes the mountain in front of us seems so large, we don't see any way around it. Or over it. Or through it. We simply want God to throw it into the sea.

When a situation arose in our household for which we desperately needed a solution, all we could do was cry out to God. As my husband and I sat in his car waiting to have a hard conversation on the phone with family members, we prayed, "Lord, we just need you to show up."

The next moment, lifting our heads from prayer, we saw a shimmering rainbow over the pond we were facing. Just a piece; not even the full arc. But we knew in that moment that God heard us, and that He was with us. We could only gaze in wonder at what God was showing us, and trust that our situation was in His loving hands.

—Stephanie Reeves

Lord, fill my eyes with Your wonders so that I never doubt that You will take care of what concerns me. Amen.

Words to Pray On

You shall not be afraid of them but you shall remember what the Lord your God did to Pharaoh and to all Egypt, the great trials that your eyes saw, the signs, the wonders, the mighty hand, and the outstretched arm, by which the Lord your God brought you out. So will the Lord your God do to all the peoples of whom you are afraid.
—Deuteronomy 7:18–19 (ESV)

But Jesus looked at them and said, "With man this is impossible, but with God all things are possible."
—Matthew 19:26 (ESV)

You are the God who works wonders; you have made known your might among the peoples.
—Psalm 77:14 (ESV)

day 33

harmony

Challenged to define music during his study as a music major, my husband came up with "a combination of sounds and/or silences arranged in such a manner as to cause some kind of an emotional impact." I like that definition, because it leaves room for the understanding that discord and harmony each have that impact.

You could apply that same idea to life itself. Instead of looking for balance in life—activities and quiet times, work and play—look for harmony. An orchestra does not have an equal number of each instrument, just as life does not have equal minutes for each role we play.

Balance strives for a single state of being, while harmony provides a range of possibilities. Balance requires perfection and being still; harmony allows for measurable movement and ongoing hope.

I believe that we're happier when we accept the discord in life. As life's tune plays on, that discord can resolve into pleasing harmony again. Listen. And take your place as the conductor of your symphony.

—Julie Holzmann

Lord, help me to live a life of harmony.

Words to Pray On

Dear brothers and sisters, I close my letter with these last words: Be joyful. Grow to maturity. Encourage each other. Live in harmony and peace. Then the God of love and peace will be with you.
—2 Corinthians 13:11 (NLT)

How wonderful and pleasant it is when brothers live together in harmony!
—Psalm 133:1 (NLT)

May God, who gives this patience and encouragement, help you live in complete harmony with each other, as is fitting for followers of Christ Jesus. Then all of you can join together with one voice, giving praise and glory to God, the Father of our Lord Jesus Christ.
—Romans 15:5–6 (NLT)

_____

_____

_____

_____

_____

day 34

cracks

My wife and I used to put our children to bed with a blessing: "May the Almighty God, the Father, the Son, and the Holy Spirit bless you and keep you." Then, after speaking their full name, we'd say, "child of the covenant," and tell them we loved them. We hoped they would go to sleep.

Sometimes, distracted, we would forget. Then we would hear: "Dad, Mom, come bless me." Such blessing speaks deeply to our hearts.

Note that in the scripture from Numbers on the opposite page, God told the priests to bless the Israelites by putting His name *on* them—not *in* them. A rabbi once explained to me: "When our heads butt against obstacles of life, we get cracks. Then those blessings that have been put *on* us seep *in* like a healing salve."

—Stephen D. Bostrom

God, You are the true source of blessings. When I am cracked by life, seep in.

Words to Pray On

The LORD said to Moses, "Tell Aaron and his sons, 'This is how you are to bless the Israelites. Say to them: "The LORD bless you and keep you; the LORD make his face shine on you and be gracious to you; the LORD turn his face toward you and give you peace."' So they will put my name on the Israelites, and I will bless them."

—Numbers 6:22–27 (NIV)

The Lord had said...."I will make you into a great nation, and I will bless you; I will make your name great, and you will be a blessing. I will bless those who bless you, and whoever curses you I will curse; and all peoples on earth will be blessed through you."

—Genesis 12:1–3 (NIV)

day 35

friends

My family and I were sitting in the bleachers of Camp Nou, a football stadium in Barcelona, when the world-famous soccer player Lionel Messi scored his team's six-thousandth goal. We immediately leapt to our feet and cheered with the uproarious crowd.

God knows I'm not an avid follower of soccer (I do like to watch the occasional game!), but having the privilege to experience that moment beside Barcelona's faithful fans was powerful. What was even more powerful, however, was getting to witness it with my very best friends: my sisters and my cousins. Seeing their faces full of shock, awe, and excitement was something I'll never forget.

That evening in Camp Nou is a lasting reminder that life is so much better—and more beautiful—with friends. And I thank God every day for giving me such good ones, and for filling my life with their laughter and joy.

—Roma Maitlall

Thank You, Lord, for blessing me with loving, lifelong friends who always make me smile and revive my hope.

Words to Pray On

Jonathan said to David, "Go in peace, for we have sworn friendship with each other in the name of the Lord, saying, 'The Lord is witness between you and me, and between your descendants and my descendants forever.'"

—1 Samuel 20:42 (NIV)

The Lord would speak to Moses face to face, as one speaks to a friend.

—Exodus 33:11 (NIV)

A friend loves at all times, and a brother is born for a time of adversity.

—Proverbs 17:17 (NIV)

_____
_____
_____
_____
_____
_____
_____

day 36

bottles

Years ago, I was strolling through a garden and came upon a bottle tree. The gardener had taken a dead tree and put colored bottles on the branches. The way the sunlight caught the colored glass made a lovely display. A sign said that the bottle tree came from an old African legend that during the night, evil spirits go into the bottles and get trapped. When the morning sun comes, they burn away.

I loved this yard decoration so much, not only because it was pretty, but also because I considered it a metaphor for Lamentations 3:22 (see opposite page). So when my Majestic Beauty Indian Hawthorn died, I made a bottle tree from its branches.

Like those colored bottles, we are vessels, transparent to God. During a day or night, we can harbor negative thoughts or feelings, but when we hold them up to the sunlight of God's love, they become fleeting.

—Nancy Schrock

Lord, help me to remember to hope in the future because Your compassion is new every morning.

Words to Pray On

Because of the Lord's great love we are not consumed, for his compassions never fail. They are new every morning; great is your faithfulness. I say to myself, "The Lord is my portion; therefore I will wait for him."
—Lamentations 3:22–24 (NIV)

For the Lord God is a sun and shield; the Lord bestows favor and honor; no good thing does he withhold from those whose walk is blameless.
—Psalm 84:11 (NIV)

The path of the righteous is like the morning sun, shining ever brighter till the full light of day.
—Proverbs 4:18 (NIV)

day 37

sustain

God has seen fit to bless me with a body that seems strong on the outside but is riddled with physical illness and weakness. Even so, it's through those weaknesses that I've discovered just how deeply God sustains me.

At seventeen, diabetes joined my life, and my journey with autoimmune illnesses began. I was told I'd be blind by forty and never have children. Fast-forward many decades, and God has been faithful to sustain me through three healthy pregnancies and no issues with my sight. The journey has not been easy; it has been riddled with pain and difficulties I never wanted, but there has never been a day where God didn't carry me.

He holds all of His children and holds us together. We are safe and sustained in His arms.

—Amy Wallace

Lord, sustain me and hold me close. I know You care for me. Amen.

Words to Pray On

Lord, sustain me as you promised, that I may live! Do not let my hope be crushed. Sustain me, and I will be rescued; then I will meditate continually on your decrees.
—Psalm 119:116–117 (NLT)

But in your great mercy you did not abandon them to die in the wilderness.... You sent your good Spirit to instruct them, and you did not stop giving them manna from heaven or water for their thirst. For forty years you sustained them in the wilderness, and they lacked nothing.
—Nehemiah 9:19–21 (NLT)

The Son radiates God's own glory and expresses the very character of God, and he sustains everything by the mighty power of his command.
—Hebrews 1:3 (NLT)

_____
_____
_____
_____
_____

day 38

be

I've always been a doer. I find great fulfillment in being busy and checking off accomplishments each day. So when illness limited how much I could do, I began to feel worthless. This verse became a frequent meditation for me. I would recite His invitation: "Be still, and know that I am God." Then as I sat in that stillness, I'd focus on specific phrases: "Be still and know that I am." Then, "Be still and know." Then, "Be still." And finally, simply, "Be."

This practice reminded me that He has already accomplished my salvation and I can rest in Him. He loves me regardless of what I can do, and I have worth to Him by simply being.

—Sharon Hinck

Lord, thank You for inviting me to be still today, even in my restless striving. Remind me that I can rest in You and simply be. Amen.

Words to Pray On

He says, "Be still, and know that I am God; I will be exalted among the nations, I will be exalted in the earth."
—Psalm 46:10 (NIV)

Moses answered the people, "Do not be afraid. Stand firm and you will see the deliverance the Lord will bring you today. The Egyptians you see today you will never see again. The Lord will fight for you; you need only to be still."
—Exodus 14:13–14 (NIV)

Now then, stand still and see this great thing the Lord is about to do before your eyes!
—1 Samuel 12:16 (NIV)

Be still before the Lord and wait patiently for him; do not fret when people succeed in their ways, when they carry out their wicked schemes.
—Psalm 37:7 (NIV)

_____

_____

_____

_____

day 39

bonds

As a teenager, my son shunned me for more than two years because I'd divorced his father. The separation broke my heart. After we reconnected, I wrote an article to encourage other estranged moms. The story led three women to email their painful stories to me. In their honor, I started a blog called *Broken Bonds, Healing Hearts*.

Since then, dozens of people have contacted me, asking for prayers that their families be reconciled. I reply to every letter and post each request on my blog so others may pray, too. I've learned that when hurting hearts join hands in prayer, they lessen the pain of a broken bond.

—Sheryl Smith-Rodgers

Lord, please heal the families and friends we know who struggle with broken bonds.

Words to Pray On

Always be humble and gentle. Be patient with each other, making allowance for each other's faults because of your love. Make every effort to keep yourselves united in the Spirit, binding yourselves together with peace. For there is one body and one Spirit, just as you have been called to one glorious hope for the future.

—Ephesians 4:2–4 (NLT)

God decided in advance to adopt us into his own family by bringing us to himself through Jesus Christ. This is what he wanted to do, and it gave him great pleasure.

—Ephesians 1:5 (NLT)

day 40

shout

My children had no qualms about shouting. When they needed something, they amplified their request by raising their voices. When they won an award, discovered something new, or found the answer to a math problem, they let everyone know. When they witnessed their first snowfall or a shooting star, the glow began on their face, moved throughout their bodies, and culminated in exuberance. The volume of their joy screamed in comparison, evident to all those around them and perhaps to the surrounding counties.

As adults, we may not always shout good news or fill the earth with singing, except on Sunday mornings. But if I could practice shouting my prayers with childlike joy, I imagine the heavens would answer in kind and sing along with me, shouting their praise to God.

—Patricia Tiffany Morris

Lord, may I be uninhibited as a child experiencing the world and learn to shout the name of Jesus to all I meet. Amen.

Words to Pray On

Shout for joy to the Lord, all the earth, burst into jubilant song with music; make music to the Lord with the harp, with the harp and the sound of singing, with trumpets and the blast of the ram's horn—shout for joy before the Lord, the King.

—Psalm 98:4–6 (NIV)

You who bring good news to Zion, go up on a high mountain. You who bring good news to Jerusalem, lift up your voice with a shout, lift it up, do not be afraid; say to the towns of Judah, "Here is your God!"

—Isaiah 40:9 (NIV)

No misfortune is seen in Jacob, no misery observed in Israel. The Lord their God is with them; the shout of the King is among them.

—Numbers 23:21 (NIV)

day 41

determination

Life has to try hard to make it in the Sonoran Desert. I think that's why I like living here. Barrel cacti spring from scorched earth through tiny crevices in rocks. Majestic saguaros store hundreds of gallons of water to sustain them through drought. Once, I even saw a palm tree pressing through the bars of a sewer grate.

Imagine. Life springing from a cesspool to get closer to the sun.

In the harshest, worst conditions, plant life finds a way. I know God wants my life to find a way, too. This takes determination.

Not unlike you, difficult realities punctuate the time line of my story. But I worship a King who, for the sake of the joy set before Him, endured the cross. You are the joy set before Him! So am I! As such, I am determined to become mature, complete, and lacking in nothing. I am determined to get closer to the Son.

—Laurie Davies

King Jesus, You understood trauma, loneliness, and rejection. When we face trials, remind us we're becoming more like You. Amen.

Words to Pray On

Consider it pure joy, my brothers and sisters, whenever you face trials of many kinds, because you know that the testing of your faith produces perseverance. Let perseverance finish its work so that you may be mature and complete, not lacking anything.
—James 1:2–4 (NIV)

Therefore, since we have been justified through faith, we have peace with God through our Lord Jesus Christ, through whom we have gained access by faith into this grace in which we now stand. And we boast in the hope of the glory of God. Not only so, but we also glory in our sufferings, because we know that suffering produces perseverance; perseverance, character; and character, hope. And hope does not put us to shame, because God's love has been poured out into our hearts through the Holy Spirit, who has been given to us.
—Romans 5:1–5 (NIV)

day 42

redeem

One of my childhood memories is of pulling a red wagon around apartment construction sites near my home. My brother and I would gather as many soda pop bottles as we could fit in our wagon and head to the local grocery store, where we redeemed them for two cents each. Our reward was extra pocket change to buy candy and comic books.

To redeem is to buy back, and it's a beautiful picture of what God has done in our lives. While we were still living in darkness and slaves to sin, Jesus redeemed us, cleaned us up, gave us a new hope and reason for living, and adopted us into the family of God. He knows you, loves you, and calls you by name.
—Dale R. Yancy

Lord, I take great comfort in knowing that You have redeemed me and call me by name. Amen.

Words to Pray On

This is what the LORD says… "Do not fear, for I have redeemed you; I have called you by name; you are Mine!"
—Isaiah 43:1 (NASB)

Into Your hand I entrust my spirit; You have redeemed me, LORD, God of truth.
—Psalm 31:5 (NASB)

Look at my affliction and rescue me, for I have not forgotten Your Law. Plead my cause and redeem me; revive me according to Your word.
—Psalm 119:153–154 (NASB)

…our great God and Savior, Christ Jesus…gave Himself for us to redeem us from every lawless deed, and to purify for Himself a people for His own possession, eager for good deeds.
—Titus 2:13–14 (NASB)

> We must accept finite
> disappointment, but never
> lose infinite hope.
> —Martin Luther King, Jr.

day 43

if

When my friends talked about how God had given them a "word for the year" and how it had changed their lives, I prayed He'd give me a special word too. He settled the word *if* into my procrastinating heart, and it truly changed my outlook.

If is such a big little word. It introduces a conditional clause. *If* I work hard at a goal, I can achieve it. *If* I eat more fruits and vegetables, I will become healthier. *If* I read a few chapters of the Bible each day, I will reach the end of the Book and be wiser for it. Obviously, *if* I procrastinate, I will often fail. Once this simple realization lodged its way into my brain, I became motivated. I became focused. I became more successful in achieving my goals. And I also became aware of just how often God uses the powerful *if* in the Bible.

—Jessica Roach Ferguson

Lord, if I focus on pleasing You, I will glorify Your name. Amen.

Words to Pray On

...if my people, who are called by my name, will humble themselves and pray and seek my face and turn from their wicked ways, then I will hear from heaven, and I will forgive their sin and will heal their land.
—2 Chronicles 7:14 (NIV)

But if from there you seek the LORD your God, you will find him if you seek him with all your heart and with all your soul.
—Deuteronomy 4:29 (NIV)

Where can I go from your Spirit? Where can I flee from your presence? If I go up into the heavens, you are there; if I make my bed in the depths, you are there. If I rise on the wings of the dawn, if I settle on the far side of the sea, even there your hand will guide me, your right hand will hold me fast.
—Psalm 139:7–10 (NIV)

day 44

beginning

"Take a picture of our dog, Grandma," my grandson, Micah, said as he held Bentley, their brown-and-black miniature pinscher, in his arms. "Then you can remember how to draw him."

I smiled at the gentle hint as I snapped several photos.

I had recently begun sketching simple drawings of my grandchildren and texting them the pictures. Although they appreciated the thought, my grandchildren critiqued my beginning attempts at capturing their clothing, hairstyles, and pets. Even I had to admit my first sketches of Bentley looked more like big-eared rats. Rather than be discouraged at their comments, I welcomed their interest. I desire to be an adult who embraces new beginnings as I model the role of a lifelong learner—one who shows my grandchildren that it's okay to let the world see my imperfect first attempts.

Who knows? Maybe I *can* learn to draw a miniature pinscher.

—Lynne Hartke

Jesus, I give You my fear of making mistakes that keeps me from exploring new beginnings.

Words to Pray On

Instruct the wise and they will be wiser still; teach the righteous and they will add to their learning. The fear of the LORD is the beginning of wisdom, and knowledge of the Holy One is understanding.

—Proverbs 9:9–10 (NIV)

...for gaining wisdom and instruction; for understanding words of insight; for receiving instruction in prudent behavior, doing what is right and just and fair; for giving prudence to those who are simple, knowledge and discretion to the young—let the wise listen and add to their learning, and let the discerning get guidance—for understanding proverbs and parables, the sayings and riddles of the wise. The fear of the LORD is the beginning of knowledge, but fools despise wisdom and instruction.

—Proverbs 1:2–7 (NIV)

day 45

purpose

Today was one of those "I feel blue" days where I wished I could edit out the not-so-nice chapters of my life—the hurts, failures, and inadequacies. As the memories kept rising, by chance I found an old kaleidoscope packed away. I examined the bits of broken colored glass, forever changing with each twist. The inside mirror reflected the beauty and uniqueness of each piece of glass.

How easy it is for me to forget that my life is in the hands of the perfect Creator who can take the roughest of materials and turn them into a beautiful plan. I thank God for taking my broken parts and using every past circumstance—good and bad—in His mysterious way, to meticulously weave a great purpose for my life.
—Kimberly Davidson

Lord, I pray You will weave everything in my life for Your perfect purpose. Amen.

Words to Pray On

In the same way, the Spirit helps us in our weakness. We do not know what we ought to pray for, but the Spirit himself intercedes for us through wordless groans. And he who searches our hearts knows the mind of the Spirit, because the Spirit intercedes for God's people in accordance with the will of God. And we know that in all things God works for the good of those who love him, who have been called according to his purpose.

—Romans 8:26–28 (NIV)

The Lord foils the plans of the nations; he thwarts the purposes of the peoples. But the plans of the Lord stand firm forever, the purposes of his heart through all generations.

—Psalm 33:10–11 (NIV)

day 46

faithful

First, I hear a soft cry followed by a shift in the mattress, and within seconds all is silent again. More potent than fatigue, faithful love drives my wife's nighttime mothering ritual. It drives me, too, during late-night yoga ball bouncing sessions, stretches of vigilant fever monitoring, and a commitment to statue-like stillness when the baby finally falls asleep on my chest.

Like a nursing mother with her beloved infant, God commits His faithful love to you, and it will endure forever. So as you pray the word *faithful*, you can imagine yourself crawling into God's lap, the place of unending, safe, eternal love. God's faithfulness is eternal, always present in our lives. Whether you feel it every day or have sometimes struggled with times when God felt distant, today He invites you to trust Him, take His hand, and let Him rewrite your story.

—AJ Smith

Father, thank You for Your goodness. Help me to rest in Your faithful love that endures forever.

Words to Pray On

Give thanks to the Lord, for he is good; his faithful love endures forever.

—Psalm 118:29 (CSB)

With your faithful love, you will lead the people you have redeemed; you will guide them to your holy dwelling with your strength.

—Exodus 15:13 (CSB)

He will also strengthen you to the end, so that you will be blameless in the day of our Lord Jesus Christ. God is faithful; you were called by him into fellowship with his Son, Jesus Christ our Lord.

—1 Corinthians 1:8–9 (CSB)

day 47

shadow

My granddaughter Ella discovered her shadow one morning as the sun streamed through the window. When she stuck out her arm, a mysterious shape on the floor stuck out its arm. When she bobbed her head, this shape bobbed, too. She delighted in this unexpected playmate. The only time she lost her new friend was when she stepped out of the sunlight. She quickly figured out the small space on the floor where she could play with her shadow.

Although the word *shadow* carries some negative associations, it also implies a very close presence. Psalm 91 promises that when we abide in God's shadow, we will experience safety and refuge. As Ella discovered, we too must stay within the Light to find the presence and joy of God's shadow.

—Mary Hix

Help me stay within Your shadow, Loving God, so I might feel Your presence and safety. Amen.

Words to Pray On

You who live in the shelter of the Most High, who abide in the shadow of the Almighty, will say to the LORD, "My refuge and my fortress; my God, in whom I trust." For he will deliver you from the snare of the hunter and from the deadly pestilence; he will cover you with his pinions, and under his wings you will find refuge; his faithfulness is a shield and defense.
—Psalm 91:1–4 (NRSVUE)

They shall again live beneath my shadow; they shall flourish as a garden; they shall blossom like the vine; their fragrance shall be like the wine of Lebanon.
—Hosea 14:7 (NRSVUE)

day 48

treasure

The warm fleece blanket had been a special gift, but I rarely used it anymore. I paused before putting it in the cardboard box. I knew I should get rid of it. The same was true of most of the "special" items in the closet I was cleaning, but everything was too good, or too sentimental. I shook my head and placed the blanket inside. Then a nice coat. Pretty soon the box was brimming.

I posted the items on a freecycle group, and within minutes got a response. "I'm homeless and it's freezing outside," a man wrote. We arranged to meet outside the library, where he had been keeping warm while using the internet services. He gratefully accepted the whole box. My castoffs became a treasure for someone else. Not only did I organize a closet, but I was able to bless someone else in the process.

—Peggy Frezon

God, I pray that my resources may bless someone today. There is nothing I have here on earth that can compare to the treasures You have in store for me in heaven.

Words to Pray On

Jesus answered, "If you want to be perfect, go, sell your possessions and give to the poor, and you will have treasure in heaven. Then come, follow me."
—Matthew 19:21 (NIV)

The kingdom of heaven is like a treasure hidden in a field. When a man found it, he hid it again, and then in his joy went and sold all he had and bought that field.
—Matthew 13:44 (NIV)

My son, if you accept my words and store up my commands within you, turning your ear to wisdom and applying your heart to understanding—indeed, if you call out for insight and cry aloud for understanding, and if you look for it as for silver and search for it as for hidden treasure, then you will understand the fear of the Lord and find the knowledge of God.
—Proverbs 2:1–5 (NIV)

day 49

shepherd

When I failed the required math and economics classes needed for admission into the business program my freshmen year of college, my advisor suggested that I explore different career paths. When I did a personality interest inventory, the career that scored the highest was teaching.

Teaching had never been my goal. At first, I felt as though God had led me astray, but I trusted my advisor and explored the possibility. Almost twenty-five years later, I have had the opportunity to travel to conferences, meet amazing educators, facilitate professional development sessions, and advocate for the educational needs of students and families.

God used my advisor to lead me in the direction that He planned for my life. He continues to care for me like a shepherd. When I lose focus and get off track, He searches for me. He gently places me back on the right path, guides me toward His purpose for my life, and protects me from dangers seen and unseen along the journey.

—Tracie E. Morrison

Father, You are the Good Shepherd. I will obey and follow where You lead. Amen!

Words to Pray On

I am the good shepherd; I know my sheep and my sheep know me—just as the Father knows me and I know the Father—and I lay down my life for the sheep.... My sheep listen to my voice; I know them, and they follow me.

—John 10:14–15, 27 (NIV)

The Lord is my shepherd, I lack nothing. He makes me lie down in green pastures, he leads me beside quiet waters, he refreshes my soul. He guides me along the right paths for his name's sake.

—Psalm 23:1–3 (NIV)

And I will give you shepherds after my own heart, who will guide you with knowledge and understanding.

—Jeremiah 3:15 (NLT)

day 50

timing

A heartwarming story to write fell in my lap. A church friend told me about a wonderful Christian couple who had served as foster parents for decades. They only cared for newborns, typically drug-exposed ones. This husband and wife showered the babies in their care with love, and, more importantly, prayed over them.

The local newspaper turned down my article. I assumed the rejection stemmed from the piece's Christian message, but I wasn't going to water down the story's substance to get it published. *Why can't I get this published, God? The story needs to be told.*

A year or so later, I connected with a regional Christian magazine. The publisher eagerly accepted my piece on the foster parents. She not only published the article, but she chose it as a cover story and paid me. *I'm so sorry, God. Why didn't I trust Your perfect timing?*

—Alice H. Murray

Dear God, I know You have better plans for me than I can imagine. Help me to trust that Your love for me will bring those plans to fruition in Your perfect timing. Amen.

Words to Pray On

"For I know the plans I have for you," declares the Lord, "plans to prosper you and not to harm you, plans to give you hope and a future."
—Jeremiah 29:11 (NIV)

There is a time for everything, and a season for every activity under the heavens....
—Ecclesiastes 3:1 (NIV)

I remain confident of this: I will see the goodness of the Lord in the land of the living. Wait for the Lord; be strong and take heart and wait for the Lord.
—Psalm 27:13–14 (NIV)

day 51

higher

After years of dedicated prayer, worship, fellowship, and study, I arrived at a place where I felt a deep abiding peace within me—but also a certain sameness about every day. No unwelcome surprises. No unexpected drama. Nothing out of the ordinary. Work was steady, friendships were strong, and the predictability of tomorrow seemed certain. I was ready for more.

In my self-centered wisdom, I prayed a new prayer: "God, take me higher. Take me to a new level of faith, understanding, and reverence for You. Show me things. Enlighten me with fresh revelation. I want to go higher." And He answered that prayer with a lost job, a crumbling relationship, and an uncertain future. I dissolved to my hands and knees one night, crying into the floor, "Lord, I asked You to take me higher!"

And He whispered, "I AM."

—Kimberly Shumate

Father, show me the way to higher ground. Amen.

Words to Pray On

As the heavens are higher than the earth, so are my ways higher than your ways and my thoughts than your thoughts.

—Isaiah 55:9 (NIV)

Can you fathom the mysteries of God? Can you probe the limits of the Almighty? They are higher than the heavens above—what can you do? They are deeper than the depths below—what can you know? Their measure is longer than the earth and wider than the sea.

—Job 11:7–9 (NIV)

I will praise you, Lord, among the nations; I will sing of you among the peoples. For great is your love, higher than the heavens; your faithfulness reaches to the skies.

—Psalm 108:3–4 (NIV)

_____

_____

_____

_____

_____

day 52

lift

I tend to lose myself in the mystery of a starry sky. When I lift my eyes, the vastness brings closeness to God in a world that sometimes seems distant and cluttered. It reminds me that what I see around me is only a blink in His beautiful design.

Look beyond the now, beloved. See the stars glittering above? He calls them by name. He calls you by name too.

Lift your distractions, lift all those things that steal your joy, and get lost in His majesty. Our Heavenly Father's love is bigger than the sky. It's bigger than anything. When we lift our hearts to Him, He holds us close every single time.

—Tina Savant Gibson

O Father, focus my wandering thoughts today and lift up my eyes to You. Amen.

Words to Pray On

Lift up your eyes and look to the heavens: Who created all these? He who brings out the starry host one by one and calls forth each of them by name. Because of his great power and mighty strength, not one of them is missing.

—Isaiah 40:26 (NIV)

I lift up my eyes to the mountains—where does my help come from? My help comes from the Lord, the Maker of heaven and earth. He will not let your foot slip—he who watches over you will not slumber; indeed, he who watches over Israel will neither slumber nor sleep.

—Psalm 121:1–4 (NIV)

_____
_____
_____
_____
_____
_____
_____

day 53

passion

Tears flowed down my cheeks as I stood in my living room. I was alone. I would always be alone. I had been a "happily ever after" kind of girl, but nothing had turned out as I hoped. I felt duped by every romantic comedy ever released. And as a divorced single mom, I'd just come to the heartbreaking realization that no one would fix it for me. No one would sweep in. No one could be all that I needed.

Except…

As I stood, stuck in hopelessness, I finally lifted my head. I looked heavenward. I called out to Jesus. *Help me to fall in love with You. I want the real thing. I don't want religion, I long for love. Help me to see Your love and love You back with passion and joy. Please, Jesus, be my everything.*

He has become just that.

—Elsa Kok Colopy

Lord, help me fall in love with You. Make this real. I long for true passion in our relationship. Amen.

Words to Pray On

Jesus replied: "Love the Lord your God with all your heart and with all your soul and with all your mind. This is the first and greatest commandment."
—Matthew 22:37–38 (NIV)

Your love, LORD, reaches to the heavens, your faithfulness to the skies. Your righteousness is like the highest mountains, your justice like the great deep. You, LORD, preserve both people and animals. How priceless is your unfailing love, O God! People take refuge in the shadow of your wings. They feast on the abundance of your house; you give them drink from your river of delights. For with you is the fountain of life; in your light we see light. Continue your love to those who know you, your righteousness to the upright in heart.
—Psalm 36:5–10 (NIV)

day 54

refreshed

I sat down with food before me and a good friend across the table from me. We looked at each other and smiled. It had been far too long since we had been able to meet face to face. Our meal extended far beyond a traditional lunch hour as we shared the joy of being in each other's company.

As I left the restaurant I was satisfied and refreshed. The food may have satisfied the needs of my stomach, but the company had refreshed my spirit.

Is there someone whose company you find refreshing? Even if you are not able to gather face to face, perhaps you can feel that joy through a phone call or email exchange. God brings us into community, sending people into our lives who can refresh our souls. May you find company that refreshes you today.
—Emily Schlaman Larsen

God, guide me to be refreshed by the company of others this day, and lead me to bring refreshment to others. Amen.

Words to Pray On

...so that by God's will I may come to you with joy and be refreshed in your company.
—Romans 15:32 (NRSVUE)

Do not be wise in your own eyes; fear the Lord and turn away from evil. It will be a healing for your flesh and a refreshment for your body.
—Proverbs 3:7–8 (NRSVUE)

Repent, therefore, and turn to God so that your sins may be wiped out, so that times of refreshing may come from the presence of the Lord and that he may send the Messiah appointed for you, that is, Jesus.
—Acts 3:19–20 (NRSVUE)

day 55

way

After I'd walked a while with friends in the mountains, I turned to walk back alone. "See you at the cabin," I called. The left side of a fork in the road I approached looked unfamiliar. I plodded up the steep right fork and soon noticed the road dissolved into the lawn of someone's home. On the private road, I imagined a snarling guard dog.

Heart pounding, I scurried downhill. With only one bar on my cell phone, how could I call for help?

I prayed, "Father, I'm lost. Which way should I go?" I noticed road signs I'd missed before and texted my friends a photo. They rescued me.

God promises to guide us. We can ask Him to show us the way—the way to pray, respond to others, make decisions, and serve Him—and know that He will answer.

—Jeannie Waters

Father, show me the way I should go each day as I follow You. Amen.

Words to Pray On

I will instruct you and teach you in the way you should go; I will guide you with My eye.

—Psalm 32:8 (NKJV)

So Jacob went on his way, and the angels of God met him.

—Genesis 32:1 (NKJV)

And the LORD went before them by day in a pillar of cloud to lead the way, and by night in a pillar of fire to give them light, so as to go by day and night. He did not take away the pillar of cloud by day or the pillar of fire by night from before the people.

—Exodus 13:21–22 (NKJV)

day 56

radiate

As I glanced at my daughter before snapping a photo, she seemed to have something smudged above her lip. I turned her toward the light so I could wipe it away, only to realize it was just a shadow. Her raised hand had blocked the light.

How often do I experience the same illusion deep within? I raise up my mistakes like a banner and live in their shadows, convincing myself I have no right to walk in the radiant light of Christ.

Jesus did not die on the cross so I could proclaim myself unworthy and undo His sacrifice. Instead, I need to look to Him, repent, and let His grace radiate into my heart. His death and resurrection, like the strongest spotlight ever, cast such a bright light that all the shadows of my sins will be no more.

—Claire McGarry

Light of All, help me understand that Your radiant grace makes me worthy, no matter my sins. Amen.

Words to Pray On

I sought the LORD, and he answered me; he delivered me from all my fears. Those who look to him are radiant; their faces are never covered with shame.
—Psalm 34:4–5 (NIV)

And we all, who with unveiled faces contemplate the Lord's glory, are being transformed into his image with ever-increasing glory, which comes from the Lord, who is the Spirit.

—2 Corinthians 3:18 (NIV)

Cleanse me with hyssop, and I will be clean; wash me, and I will be whiter than snow.

—Psalm 51:7 (NIV)

_____
_____
_____
_____
_____
_____
_____

Hope lies in dreams, in imagination,
and in the courage of those who
dare to make dreams into reality.
—Jonas Salk

day 57

volunteers

As a girl, I learned how to crochet from a neighbor. After my first baby, I took up the craft again. Another baby came, so my crocheting dwindled.

After the kids left home, I found an afghan I'd started for my daughter. I finished it and discovered that hooking yarn soothed me. Why not continue? I searched online for charitable projects and found Warm Up America. Since 2019, I've crocheted more than one thousand acrylic sections for the nonprofit organization. Other volunteers join the pieces into blankets for people in need. All together, volunteer crocheters and knitters have made and distributed more than one million blankets! What a blessing to know that my small sections come together with others and warm countless people in a big way.

—Sheryl Smith-Rodgers

Lord, bless the volunteers who make Your world a more caring place.

Words to Pray On

You know that these hands of mine have worked to supply my own needs and even the needs of those who were with me. And I have been a constant example of how you can help those in need by working hard. You should remember the words of the Lord Jesus: "It is more blessed to give than to receive."
—Acts 20:34–35 (NLT)

Be strong and courageous, and do the work. Don't be afraid or discouraged, for the Lord God, my God, is with you.... Others with skills of every kind will volunteer, and the officials and the entire nation are at your command.
—1 Chronicles 28:20–21 (NLT)

day 58

countenance

Such a happy surprise! Stepping onto our front porch one morning, my eyes caught a glimpse of hearts drawn in colorful chalk and the letters *xoxo*. Immediately my countenance was lifted and joyful. I moved forward into my day feeling loved and inspired.

How exciting to share the love and joy of Jesus with others. Just as my children's kindness spurred my happiness that day, God uses us to spur and encourage others. That morning, I left home ready to sharpen, share, encourage, and inspire others.

It's amazing how a simple gesture of kindness can transform someone's countenance. Daily we can impact others for His kingdom. We can lovingly point our friends and family to God's Word, encourage them to deepen their relationship with Christ, and encourage a countenance of joy—just as my children did.

—Dawn Bata

Dear Father, may my words, deeds, and countenance always point others to You. Amen.

Words to Pray On

As iron sharpens iron, so a man sharpens the countenance of his friend.
—Proverbs 27:17 (NKJV)

This is the way you shall bless the children of Israel. Say to them: "The Lord bless you and keep you; the Lord make His face shine upon you, and be gracious to you; the Lord lift up His countenance upon you, and give you peace."
—Numbers 6:23–26 (NKJV)

For the Lord is righteous, He loves righteousness; His countenance beholds the upright.
—Psalm 11:7 (NKJV)

day 59

polish

Running my fingers over the rust-colored stones, I wonder how long they've been tossed by Lake Superior's waves. Years of gentle shifting on days as calm as this have rounded their edges. Yet the job seems incomplete.

Over the following weeks, I listen to the clunk-clunking of my rock tumbler. Its cadence reminds me of God's faithful work of refining my heart. Sometimes this process is gentle, like stones dancing across a lake bed. Other times, life's circumstances pluck me from that natural pace and find me in harsher conditions. The erosion of my former habits and attitudes is dialed up like stones in a tumbler.

After three weeks, I hardly recognize the stones. All their rough edges have been sanded away, revealing previously hidden beauty. They are kaleidoscopes of turquoise, orange, pink, and burgundy. Their newfound beauty reminds me that God uses every season—the gentle and the harsh—to polish my soul so that I can reflect His glory.

—Eryn Lynum

Dear Lord, thank You for polishing my heart. Help me trust Your refining hand. Amen.

Words to Pray On

Dear friends, now we are children of God, and what we will be has not yet been made known. But we know that when Christ appears, we shall be like him, for we shall see him as he is.
—1 John 3:2 (NIV)

In all this you greatly rejoice, though now for a little while you may have had to suffer grief in all kinds of trials. These have come so that the proven genuineness of your faith—of greater worth than gold, which perishes even though refined by fire—may result in praise, glory and honor when Jesus Christ is revealed.
—1 Peter 1:6–7 (NIV)

day 60

refuge

Hidden back behind a train trestle is a twenty-acre tract dappled with shade trees, a flowing creek, and a freestanding lean-to built by my stepson Ryan. It was his special place, where he went to write, draw, and rest from the world.

After his death, I found a picture of Ry sitting high up on the limb of a tree, his lean-to below him. I didn't know why, but God kept bringing that lean-to to my mind.

One day, I opened my Bible and read Psalm 62:5–7. I finally got what God was trying to show me. I had a 5 x 7 print made of that picture with those verses printed on it. It hangs on our refrigerator to remind me that, like Ryan's lean-to, God is my refuge when my grief-stricken heart is longing for rest and searching for hope.

—Amy Catlin Wozniak

Dear Lord, remind me in times of trouble You are my refuge. In times of grief, You are my hope. Amen.

Words to Pray On

Yes, my soul, find rest in God; my hope comes from him. Truly he is my rock and my salvation; he is my fortress, I will not be shaken. My salvation and my honor depend on God; he is my mighty rock, my refuge.
—Psalm 62:5–7 (NIV)

There is no one like the God of Jeshurun, who rides across the heavens to help you and on the clouds in his majesty. The eternal God is your refuge, and underneath are the everlasting arms.
—Deuteronomy 33:26–27 (NIV)

As for God, his way is perfect: The LORD's word is flawless; he shields all who take refuge in him. For who is God besides the LORD? And who is the Rock except our God?
—2 Samuel 22:31–32 (NIV)

day 61

worship

Often when something good but unexpected happens, I burst out into a song to God. "Our God is an awesome God!"

Worship can take many forms, from singing, dancing, praying, and fellowship to reading the Word. How we worship on Sunday may look different from when we are alone in our room. I find all kinds of worship suitable for connecting with God, including giving thanks or just being in His presence.

Pray the word *worship* today and think of how you can reach out, seek, and honor God. If you have access to YouTube, for example, you can search and find a song or hymn that gets your spirit moving. Play it and sing along with enthusiasm and joy! Bring a joyful song before the Lord.

—Rebecca Chamaa

Dear God, please accept all my efforts to worship and draw near to You. Help my heart fill with joy, and allow me to offer You a song!

Words to Pray On

Shout for joy to the LORD, all the earth. Worship the LORD with gladness; come before him with joyful songs. Know that the LORD is God. It is he who made us, and we are his; we are his people, the sheep of his pasture. Enter his gates with thanksgiving and his courts with praise; give thanks to him and praise his name. For the LORD is good and his love endures forever; his faithfulness continues through all generations.

—Psalm 100:1–5 (NIV)

Therefore, I urge you, brothers and sisters, in view of God's mercy, to offer your bodies as a living sacrifice, holy and pleasing to God—this is your true and proper worship.

—Romans 12:1 (NIV)

day 62

forget

My fingers hovered lightly over the black and white keys as I got my bearings. I opened the tattered pages and began to play "To a Wild Rose"—a simple piece that I'd learned when I was a teenager and hadn't played in decades. As if returning home, my fingers, my mind, and the rich notes of the piano came together in a rusty but recognizable melody.

How remarkable the human mind is! I know a bitter woman who recites in painful detail grievances she's carried for a lifetime. She sees only thorns. I know another with a smile on her face and buoyancy in her step who has learned to release the pain of her past. She inhales the fragrance of the wild rose.

—Leslie McLeod

Lord, thank You for giving us the choice to remember Your blessings and forget the former things. I'm so grateful You choose to remember my sins no more!

Words to Pray On

Forget the former things; do not dwell on the past. See, I am doing a new thing! Now it springs up; do you not perceive it? I am making a way in the wilderness and streams in the wasteland.

—Isaiah 43:18–19 (NIV)

I, even I, am he who blots out your transgressions, for my own sake, and remembers your sins no more.

—Isaiah 43:25 (NIV)

…we will tell the next generation the praiseworthy deeds of the LORD, his power, and the wonders he has done.…so the next generation would know them, even the children yet to be born, and they in turn would tell their children. Then they would put their trust in God and would not forget his deeds but would keep his commands.

—Psalm 78:4, 6–7 (NIV)

day 63

intercession

It was the day of Dad's surgery. A nurse wheeled his cot into the elevator. My two sisters and our husbands crowded in around him. I'm sure that my nervous expression mirrored theirs.

A young man in the corner of the elevator gestured toward Dad and said, "I can see that your father is very special to you."

"Yes, he is." I fought back tears.

"I'm going to pray for you and him," he said as the doors opened.

I looked back at him gratefully as I stepped out into the corridor leading to the surgical unit.

As we waited for the outcome of the surgery, my hope and faith increased, knowing that a compassionate stranger was interceding, praying to God on our behalf.

—Kristy Dewberry

Father, today I pray on behalf of others who are in need.

Words to Pray On

Therefore, confess your sins to one another and pray for one another, that you may be healed. The prayer of a righteous person has great power as it is working.
—James 5:16 (ESV)

If there is famine in the land, if there is pestilence or blight or mildew or locust or caterpillar, if their enemy besieges them in the land at their gates, whatever plague, whatever sickness there is, whatever prayer, whatever plea is made by any man...hear in heaven your dwelling place and forgive and act and render to each whose heart you know, according to all his ways (for you, you only, know the hearts of all the children of mankind).

—1 Kings 8:37–39 (ESV)

day 64

birth

After my husband and I had been married a year, we decided the time was right to add children to our family. Little did we know that it would take us more than four years for that to become a reality. Infertility was never in our plans. Those four-plus years of waiting on God were some of the hardest of my life. Month after month disappointment would come. We had no guarantees we'd ever be parents. But God was always there. He was always holding me. I didn't know whether I would ever give birth to my own child, but I never lost sight of God's goodness.

Now, more than twenty-five years later, we have three biological children. My heart is full, but honestly it was never empty—God always filled it with Himself.
—Stephanie Reeves

Father God, You fill my heart, even when it aches. You birthed hope within me by Your very presence. I am so grateful. In Jesus's name. Amen.

Words to Pray On

Hope deferred makes the heart sick, but a desire fulfilled is a tree of life.

—Proverbs 13:12 (ESV)

Yet you are he who took me from the womb; you made me trust you at my mother's breasts. On you was I cast from my birth, and from my mother's womb you have been my God.

—Psalm 22:9–10 (ESV)

And you will have joy and gladness, and many will rejoice at his birth, for he will be great before the Lord.

—Luke 1:14–15 (ESV)

day 65

heighten

Every morning, sometime between 8 and 8:30, my dogs bark wildly. What sets them off? A Saint Bernard and his person walking by our house. From a human perspective, there's absolutely no reason they should know it's him. The Saint Bernard doesn't bark. His people are calm, normal humans. My dogs can't see them. But they know he's there.

It's not superpowers, but their heightened senses. Listening for the faintest sound. Smelling the air. Watching for shadows or movement. The faithfulness of these morning walks. They accept what they cannot see.

And so it can be for us. We may not see God, but we can know He's there. Watch for Him to move. Listen for His voice. Recall His faithfulness. Feel His presence. Even if we can't explain it. Because God, in all His magnificent glory, is not easily explained. He simply is.

—April Kidwell

Lord, I want to know You are with me. Heighten my senses. I want to watch, listen, and recall. Help me know You are near.

Words to Pray On

Be strong and courageous. Do not be afraid; do not be discouraged, for the Lord your God will be with you wherever you go.

—Joshua 1:9 (NIV)

The Lord said to him, "Who gave human beings their mouths? Who makes them deaf or mute? Who gives them sight or makes them blind? Is it not I, the Lord? Now go; I will help you speak and teach you what to say."

—Exodus 4:11–12 (NIV)

You are my strength, I watch for you; you, God, are my fortress, my God on whom I can rely.

—Psalm 59:9–10 (NIV)

_____

_____

_____

_____

_____

_____

day 66

write

My oldest child of four, Jeremy, moved out of our home as a college sophomore. I struggled with the move, even though it was just across town, closer to the university, and in my mom's backyard. My mother gave permission for Jeremy and two friends to live in his grandmother's double-wide trailer, left vacant when she'd passed away years before. The trailer's porch needed a fresh paint job, but otherwise would meet the needs of three college boys.

While Jeremy served in a mission experience over the summer before he moved in, his three younger siblings and I helped my mom paint the screened-in porch. But first, we used pencils to write Bible verses on each of the boards framing it. Something about surrounding Jeremy with God's Word gave me a sense of peace. I knew I'd still miss him, but I no longer worried about his exit from our home.

—Julie Lavender

God, when I worry or fret, please remind me to read Your word, write Your word, speak Your word, pray Your word—whatever it takes to surround me with Your comfort. Amen.

Words to Pray On

Fix these words of mine in your hearts and minds; tie them as symbols on your hands and bind them on your foreheads. Teach them to your children, talking about them when you sit at home and when you walk along the road, when you lie down and when you get up. Write them on the doorframes of your houses and on your gates, so that your days and the days of your children may be...as many as the days that the heavens are above the earth.

—Deuteronomy 11:18–21 (NIV)

We proclaim to you what we have seen and heard, so that you also may have fellowship with us. And our fellowship is with the Father and with his Son, Jesus Christ. We write this to make our joy complete.

—1 John 1:3–4 (NIV)

day 67

sunrise

Blessed by an unobstructed view to the east, I stand each dawn in awed anticipation of the rising of the sun. The sky may be ablaze with orange, pink, gold, and coral, or awash with grey and blue. Regardless, my heart swells with joy at the brilliant edge of sun peaking above the horizon and its emergence into radiant fullness. I thank God for His gift of a new day.

Sunrise symbolizes peace, restoration, a new beginning. No matter if yesterday held disappointment, sadness, failure. Sunrise brings hope—a fresh chance, a clear slate, a reminder that God stands ready to forgive, forget, and start anew. The rising of the sun, as the rising of the Son, is certain, powerful, and glorious. It promises hope to me—to all the world.

When I feel exhausted, discouraged, disappointed, defeated, I whisper my prayer of "sunrise" and am reminded that with God, our hope is eternal.
—Kim Taylor Henry

Lord God, "sunrise." Thank You for reminding me every day that with You, I always have hope.

Words to Pray On

But for you who revere my name, the sun of righteousness will rise with healing in its rays.
—Malachi 4:2 (NIV)

God came from Teman, the Holy One from Mount Paran. His glory covered the heavens and his praise filled the earth. His splendor was like the sunrise; rays flashed from his hand, where his power was hidden.
— Habakkuk 3:3–4 (NIV)

The Mighty One, God, the Lord, speaks and summons the earth from the rising of the sun to where it sets.
—Psalm 50:1 (NIV)

day 68

sparrow

Because of my love for animals, my parents wouldn't allow me to watch *Lassie* when I was a child. I'd cry when Lassie got lost and was upset when Lassie was in trouble at an episode's end.

On vacation one summer when I was a teen, I found a small bird who couldn't fly. I rescued and took care of it. When the time came to return home, I was distraught about leaving the bird to die. Dad located a wildlife rescue center nearby and drove me there to leave the bird before we departed.

If I can be so concerned about a fictional dog and a tiny bird, just think how much our Heavenly Father cares about us. He is so loving that even a wee sparrow doesn't fall without His notice—and likely a tug at His heart. How much more is His concern for His children?

—Alice H. Murray

Dear God, thank You for Your loving care for all living things. Amen.

Words to Pray On

Are not two sparrows sold for a penny? Yet not one of them fall to the ground outside your Father's care. And even the very hairs of your head are all numbered. So don't be afraid; you are worth more than many sparrows.

—Matthew 10:29–31 (NIV)

Even the sparrow has found a home, and the swallow a nest for herself, where she may have her young—a place near your altar, Lord Almighty, my King and my God. Blessed are those who dwell in your house; they are ever praising you.

—Psalm 84:3–4 (NIV)

_____

_____

_____

_____

_____

_____

_____

day 69

because

My family has a tradition of giving gifts for no particular occasion—not for birthdays, Christmas, or other life events, but just because we love them. We call them "just because" presents.

One afternoon my four-year-old niece came in from playing outside. Both hands were behind her back. As soon as she walked through the door, she presented me with a bouquet of tiny violets picked from my yard. "Because," she said excitedly, and smiled. That one word oozed with love and warmed my heart. I winked and replied, "Because."

Because is such a perfect one-word prayer. Because—I need His help. Because—He never fails me. Because—He is greater than any problem. Because—His will is perfect. Because—I cannot do life without Him. Because—I love Him and He loves me.

—Nyla Kay Wilkerson

Dear Father, because I need You every minute of every day, I pray to You. Amen.

Words to Pray On

Whoever does not love does not know God, for God is love.

—1 John 4:8 (GNT)

"But now I will come," says the Lord, "because the needy are oppressed and the persecuted groan in pain. I will give them the security they long for."

—Psalm 12:5 (GNT)

Whoever welcomes God's messenger because he is God's messenger, will share in his reward. And whoever welcomes a good man because he is good, will share in his reward. You can be sure that whoever gives even a drink of cold water to one of the least of these my followers because he is my follower, will certainly receive a reward.

—Matthew 10:41–42 (GNT)

day 70

Jesus

"Momma, I'm scared," seven-year-old me cried out in the darkness.

Momma came running. "Say *Jesus*," she comforted. "He's the *way* through fear."

"I'm worthless," twenty-five-year-old me confessed to a friend. "I'll never amount to anything."

Shaking her head, she exhorted, "Proclaim *Jesus*. He'll speak *truth* to that lie, even though believing may take time."

"Sometimes I feel dead inside," forty-eight-year-old me complained to my husband. "Where's the joy I once knew?"

And he held me. "Whisper *Jesus*, dear. His very name holds *life*, reminding you of the joy of your salvation."

After all these years, I'm a believer. In the varying seasons of our days, simply yet profoundly praying the name *Jesus* will serve to offer life in the face of figurative and even literal death.

Jesus—yes!

—Maureen Miller

Jesus. Jesus. Jesus. Amen.

Words to Pray On

"Do not let your hearts be troubled. You believe in God; believe also in me.... You know the way to the place where I am going." Thomas said to him, "Lord, we don't know where you are going, so how can we know the way?" Jesus answered, "I am the way and the truth and the life. No one comes to the Father except through me. If you really know me, you will know my Father as well. From now on, you do know him and have seen him."

—John 14:1, 4–7 (NIV)

The Word became flesh and made his dwelling among us. We have seen his glory, the glory of the one and only Son, who came from the Father, full of grace and truth.

—John 1:14 (NIV)

_____

_____

_____

_____

_____

"Hope" is the thing with feathers that perches in the soul—and sings the tune without the words—and never stops at all.
—Emily Dickinson

day 71

peace

As we neared retirement, we wondered what the call of God would be in the concluding chapter of our lives. With open hearts, we visited a church in the town where we hoped to live.

"Peace to this house," the preacher began. "It's an old Aramaic blessing."

The text was from Luke 10, the story of Jesus sending out His disciples to teach and heal. When the preacher pointed out that the heart of the disciples' call was to bring peace wherever they went, both of us recognized the whisper of the Spirit's voice echoing in our ears.

Today the words are framed in our entryway, calligraphed by a friend, reminding us each time the doorbell rings of our call to bring peace. We welcome each visitor as Christ. We reach out to neighbors and friends, inviting them for meals and conversation. And when tensions emerge, as they inevitably do, we practice listening and ask questions, rather than take sides.
—Marlene Kropf

God of peace, bless each friend and neighbor whom I meet today. Amen.

Words to Pray On

Whatever house you enter, first say, "Peace to this house!"

—Luke 10:5 (NRSVUE)

Let me hear what God the Lord will speak, for he will speak peace to his people, to his faithful, to those who turn to him in their hearts.

—Psalm 85:8 (NRSVUE)

Above all, clothe yourselves with love, which binds everything together in perfect harmony. And let the peace of Christ rule in your hearts, to which indeed you were called in one body. And be thankful. Let the word of Christ dwell in you richly; teach and admonish one another in all wisdom; and with gratitude in your hearts sing psalms, hymns, and spiritual songs to God.

—Colossians 3:14–16 (NRSVUE)

day 72

creation

I learn much from the beauty of the natural world. The golden orb of the sun rising over the horizon points to a God who watches over us with tender eyes. The expansive sky reminds me that though Earth is a small dot in a large universe, our existence is known and desired.

Rains proclaim that sorrow is part of life, softening the hard earth of my heart, making way for joy and growth. Snowfalls, a paradox of pristine wonder and numbing cold, suggest that life is complex and nuanced. Oceans speak of God's deep mercy and love.

Flowers, briefly clothed in exquisite beauty and dazzling colors, trumpet songs of exuberance. Stately, majestic trees transform from rich shades of green to vibrant reds and golds, sparkling like jewels in all seasons.

When I survey the forests, oceans, and skies, I am touched by what God teaches me through this beautiful world.

—Prasanta Verma

Dear Lord, please help me to be mindful of what You teach me through this beautifully created world.

Words to Pray On

The heavens declare the glory of God; the skies proclaim the work of his hands. Day after day they pour forth speech; night after night they reveal knowledge.
—Psalm 19:1–2 (NIV)

You alone are the LORD. You made the heavens, even the highest heavens, and all their starry host, the earth and all that is on it, the seas and all that is in them. You give life to everything, and the multitudes of heaven worship you.

—Nehemiah 9:6 (NIV)

Where is God my Maker, who gives songs in the night, who teaches us more than he teaches the beasts of the earth and makes us wiser than the birds in the sky?

—Job 35:10–11 (NIV)

day 73

music

Once, while vacationing in Rome, my family and I found ourselves in the famous Piazza Navona—and felt as if we had stepped into heaven.

There we were, standing in the middle of the ancient square, while a street band performed a breathtaking rendition of Johann Pachelbel's famous "Canon in D Major." The music sounded otherworldly.

Then, as one musician expertly strummed a cello and another played a violin, a nearby hawker began blowing bubbles. I watched in awe as the glossy orbs floated across the cloudless, blue sky—a fitting backdrop to the heavenly music surrounding me.

That wondrous summer day taught me that music is truly a gift from God. It revives and refreshes the soul, filling it with the assurance that God is everywhere—even in the notes of a song. Whenever you feel down, put on your favorite piece of music. I am sure you will feel instantly uplifted.

—Roma Maitlall

Heavenly Father, when I feel sad, fill my body and soul with the music of Your heavenly choir.

Words to Pray On

Sing and make music from your heart to the Lord, always giving thanks to God the Father for everything, in the name of our Lord Jesus Christ.
—Ephesians 5:19–20 (NIV)

My heart, O God, is steadfast, my heart is steadfast; I will sing and make music. Awake, my soul! Awake, harp and lyre! I will awaken the dawn.
—Psalm 57:7–8 (NIV)

The trumpeters and musicians joined in unison to give praise and thanks to the Lord. Accompanied by trumpets, cymbals and other instruments, the singers raised their voices in praise to the Lord and sang: "He is good; his love endures forever."
—2 Chronicles 5:13 (NIV)

day 74

cultivate

"I'll never have a green thumb like Mom," I remember saying after killing another set of baby plants I'd grown from seed. Year after year, I would plant something with the kids—a few tomato plants, herbs, or flowers. They'd flourish for a bit, then they died. So I began to think, *Oh, I just can't grow anything.* But I was wrong about that.

Each year, I've noticed how the plants have started to stick around a little longer. What made the difference? When I tended to them a bit more by taking time to care for them, making sure to water them as instructed, and paying attention to the needed sunlight instruction, they did well. They needed to be cultivated.

And so it is with us. We must cultivate our relationship with God if we expect it to grow and to maintain a healthy spiritual life. Even if we don't think we have a green thumb, we might be surprised at what happens when we pay attention to the instructions.

—Natasha N. Smith

Lord, help me to take time each day to cultivate my relationship with You. Amen.

Words to Pray On

He makes grass grow for the cattle, and plants for people to cultivate—bringing forth food from the earth...oil to make their faces shine, and bread that sustains their hearts.
—Psalm 104:14–15 (NIV)

This is what the Sovereign Lord says: On the day I cleanse you from all your sins, I will resettle your towns, and the ruins will be rebuilt. The desolate land will be cultivated instead of lying desolate in the sight of all who pass through it. They will say, "This land that was laid waste has become like the garden of Eden..."
—Ezekiel 36:33–35 (NIV)

day 75

laughter

Recently, I gave the devotion at our once-a-month church breakfast. I wore a new pair of slacks. You're familiar with that clear strip on the front of the pant leg showing your size? It wasn't on the front this time. Everyone to my left had a clear view of my size. When my friend Lisa and I met after Sunday school class to pray for the church service, her eyes grew round and she pointed. The only thing she could say is "Oh." I laughed as if I wore stickers on my leg every day.

My husband is fond of saying, "After every success, we experience a failure." Well, that failure came quick!

I couldn't help but think of ninety-year-old Sarah laughing when God told Abraham she would get pregnant: Sarah said, "God has brought me laughter, and everyone who hears about this will laugh with me" (Genesis 21:6, NIV).

—Jessica Roach Ferguson

Thank You, Lord, for keeping me grounded and in my place, and giving me (and my audience, if they noticed) humor. Amen.

Words to Pray On

Our mouths were filled with laughter, our tongues with songs of joy. Then it was said among the nations, "The LORD has done great things for them." The LORD has done great things for us, and we are filled with joy.
—Psalm 126:2–3 (NIV)

A wife of noble character who can find? She is worth far more than rubies.... She is clothed with strength and dignity; she can laugh at the days to come.
—Proverbs 31:10, 25 (NIV)

Blessed are you who are poor, for yours is the kingdom of God. Blessed are you who hunger now, for you will be satisfied. Blessed are you who weep now, for you will laugh.

—Luke 6:20–21 (NIV)

day 76

cease

"Stand next to the lamppost," I said to my sister, Renae, as I snapped a picture at sunset on London Bridge. We were not visiting England, however, but Lake Havasu, Arizona. The famous bridge had been sold by the City of London after it became too structurally unsound to handle modern traffic, and it had been brought across the Atlantic and reassembled block by block over a stretch of the Colorado River in the 1970s. The ornate lampposts caught our attention. They had been created from the melted cannons of Napoleon Bonaparte's defeated army after the battle of Waterloo, a powerful symbol of the peace and light that come when fighting ends and wars cease.

As the last rays of sunlight turned the sky a brilliant orange, I whispered a prayer for the ending of current wars and conflicts causing destruction and mayhem. For conflicts within my own heart and mind. *May they cease.* For battles in relationships. *Cease.* For countries warring over territory. *Cease.* For people acting against other human beings. *Cease.*

—Lynne Hartke

Jesus, may all situations distorted by war and conflict cease. Amen.

Words to Pray On

He makes wars cease to the end of the earth; he breaks the bow and shatters the spear; he burns the chariots with fire.

—Psalm 46:9 (ESV)

And a great windstorm arose, and the waves were breaking into the boat, so that the boat was already filling. But he was in the stern, asleep on the cushion. And they woke him and said to him, "Teacher, do you not care that we are perishing?" And he awoke and rebuked the wind and said to the sea, "Peace! Be still!" And the wind ceased, and there was a great calm.

—Mark 4:37–39 (ESV)

day 77

unfurl

Recently I was exploring a wooded path near our home. The trail was just turning green with new life. I bent down to examine a young fern.

Have you ever noticed the way a fern grows? Tiny fronds appear at the base of the stem. The top is tightly wound, resembling the neck and scroll of a fiddle. As the fern matures, the top gently unfurls and the fronds spread open, fully stretching to soak in the sun. That's the way that I have matured in my spiritual walk. I started off closed tight, unsure of what to believe. As I studied, I began to grow and open myself up to the Word.

There, beside the fern, I stood, raised my eyes to the sky, and extended my arms. When I'm outstretched like this, I can fully soak in the Son.

—Peggy Frezon

God, You have given me a banner of strength, and I unfurl it as You plant Your Spirit in me, and I grow.

Words to Pray On

But for those who fear you, you have raised a banner to be unfurled against the bow.

—Psalm 60:4 (NIV)

Moses replied, "When I have gone out of the city, I will spread out my hands in prayer to the Lord. The thunder will stop and there will be no more hail, so you may know that the earth is the Lord's."

—Exodus 9:29 (NIV)

I remember the days of long ago; I meditate on all your works and consider what your hands have done. I spread out my hands to you; I thirst for you like a parched land.

—Psalm 143:5–6 (NIV)

day 78

present

It was a cold morning as I pulled into the fog-covered parking lot when a nearby car caught my eye—a rust-streaked, matte grey hatchback with a giant bumper sticker plastered across the back: *I'd rather be here now.* I was surprised, even impressed. I often find myself looking to the future while squirming in the present.

Perhaps you, too, feel the future pulling you from the present moment. However, the present moment is where God has you. It's where your life is. So, therefore, as you pray the word *present*, ask yourself, "How is God coming to me here and now?" God isn't waiting for you tomorrow. God is right here, right now, in the present.

—AJ Smith

Lord, help me be here with You, right here, right now.

Words to Pray On

Therefore do not worry about tomorrow, for tomorrow will worry about itself. Each day has enough trouble of its own.

—Matthew 6:34 (NIV)

God again set a certain day, calling it "Today."

—Hebrews 4:7 (NIV)

He began by saying to them, "Today this scripture is fulfilled in your hearing."

—Luke 4:21 (NIV)

Then he said, "Jesus, remember me when you come into your kingdom." Jesus answered him, "Truly I tell you, today you will be with me in paradise."

—Luke 23:42–43 (NIV)

day 79

unsubscribe

My daughter noticed the high number floating over the mail icon on my phone. "Mom—8,256 unread emails!? What's the point?" Later, on a long car trip while my husband drove, I started deleting mail. Then I realized I needed to unsubscribe from junk email lists, not just delete individual emails. Discount wedding supplies? Unsubscribe. A gloom and doom political newsletter? Unsubscribe. Vegan dietary supplements? Unsubscribe.

Could I also unsubscribe from all the mental junk that clogs my mind? *My value depends on how I look.* Unsubscribe. *My husband does it just to annoy me.* Unsubscribe. *God can never fix this mess.* Unsubscribe.

What would I be like if I changed the stinking thinking I so often subscribed to? Instead, I can choose to unsubscribe. Then I can choose to think on things that are true, honorable, and pleasing. How much more lovely my mental inbox and my behavior will be!

—Mary Hix

Loving God, help me to unsubscribe from lies and distortions and to choose to think on the excellence of Your truth. Amen.

Words to Pray On

Finally, brothers and sisters, whatever is true, whatever is honorable, whatever is just, whatever is pure, whatever is pleasing, whatever is commendable, if there is any excellence and if there is anything worthy of praise, think about these things.
—Philippians 4:8 (NRSVUE)

Awake, awake, clothe yourself in your strength, Zion; clothe yourself with your beautiful garments.... Shake yourself from the dust, rise up, captive Jerusalem; release yourself from the chains around your neck, captive daughter of Zion.
—Isaiah 52:1–2 (NASB)

We destroy arguments and every proud obstacle raised up against the knowledge of God, and we take every thought captive to obey Christ.
—2 Corinthians 10:4–5 (NRSVUE)

day 80

majesty

While camping in the Everglades in Big Cypress Preserve, I went walking just after sunset. Flashlight off, with no man-made lights in sight, I couldn't see my feet on the path. Stars and constellations too numerous to count speckled a black sky in every direction. I stood marveling at this glimpse of the wonder of God's great majesty, power, and glory. He made all this with a single command. *Do you see now what I created? You can handle the passing of two family members, soured relationships, hurricanes, fires, war, and rumors of war. These tragedies touch your life, but remember that you have a great God who will never leave or forsake you.*

At 5:00 a.m., I opened my eyes and looked out the camper back window. Light slowly emerged from under a bank of clouds signaling a new day. My heart filled with thankfulness. I'd witnessed the day's end, plus a brand-new day dawning—a fresh start and a new beginning.

—Teresa K. Lasher

Lord, may I continue to marvel at Your majesty every day in every way. Amen.

Words to Pray On

LORD, our LORD, how majestic is Your name in all the earth, You who have displayed Your splendor above the heavens!

—Psalm 8:1 (NASB)

Yours, LORD, is the greatness, the power, the glory, the victory, and the majesty, indeed everything that is in the heavens and on the earth; Yours is the dominion, LORD, and You exalt Yourself as head over all. Both riches and honor come from You, and You rule over all, and in Your hand is power and might; and it lies in Your hand to make great and to strengthen everyone.

—1 Chronicles 29:11–12 (NASB)

day 81

angels

The street was lit by one lonely lamppost. Beyond it, the blackness of the park embraced its nightly gathering of homeless, drug dealers, and drifters. Earlier, my friend had warned me, "Don't go there after dark. It's not safe!" I'm not naïve or careless, but I knew in my heart that I was the only one who could find him and make the special delivery.

As I entered, I saw the shadowed silhouettes of people huddled in small groups. Some were sitting, some standing, others wandering around. Then I felt a presence behind me, following me. I turned. Two policemen smiled as they escorted me, stride for stride, across the grass. I smiled back. Then I heard my name. It was John, a man I had met downtown that day. I handed him a Bible, and we hugged.

When I turned to leave seconds later—the policemen were nowhere in sight.

—Kimberly Shumate

Father, I pray that Your angels stay close to me everywhere I go, whether I'm aware of them or not. Amen.

Words to Pray On

...some have welcomed angels as guests without knowing it.

—Hebrews 13:2 (CSB)

I am going to send an angel before you to protect you on the way and bring you to the place I have prepared.

—Exodus 23:20 (CSB)

No harm will come to you; no plague will come near your tent. For he will give his angels orders concerning you, to protect you in all your ways.

—Psalm 91:10–11 (CSB)

day 82

bride

In my early days as a young Christian, Jeremiah 2:2 held special significance for me. As a young, unmarried woman, I understood the concept of being a bride and all the promises that marriage entailed. Now, after forty-three years of wedlock and forty-five years of walking with the Lord, I don't look or feel like a bride anymore. My skin is wrinkled, and my hair is gray.

But I believe Jesus still thinks of me as His bride, loving Him and following Him through the wilderness, and this verse always brings me back to the beginning of my adventure of learning to follow the Lord. I didn't know what lay ahead, but I trusted Him to lead me through it. Today, I remember the devotion of my youth and reclaim some of the simple innocence of following the Lord through a land not sown.

—Renee Yancy

Thank You, Lord, for making me Your bride. Please continue to teach me to follow You through lands not yet sown.

Words to Pray On

This is what the Lord says: "I remember the devotion of your youth, how as a bride you loved me and followed me through the wilderness, through a land not sown."
—Jeremiah 2:2 (NIV)

I delight greatly in the Lord; my soul rejoices in my God. For he has clothed me with garments of salvation and arrayed me in a robe of his righteousness, as a bridegroom adorns his head like a priest, and as a bride adorns herself with her jewels.
—Isaiah 61:10 (NIV)

As a young man marries a young woman, so will your Builder marry you; as a bridegroom rejoices over his bride, so will your God rejoice over you.
—Isaiah 62:5 (NIV)

day 83

dirt

This has been a dirty spring. We've had three major dirt storms, one so severe it caused a blackout similar to those in the 1930s. My windows are spattered with the dirt that blew in immediately after a light rain shower. My dog Pepper tracks dried grass and dirt onto the porch several times a day. Dirt seeps in under the doors, and don't even mention trying to keep things dusted!

But as I was sweeping, it occurred to me that dirt has its blessings. The spotted windows mean that our drought-stricken area received a bit of rain. Dirt on Pepper's paws reminds me I'm grateful for her companionship. As I watch a tractor kick up dirt in the field by my house, I picture the corn crop we'll have this fall. And I praise God for the earth's dirt in this world He created.

—Penney Schwab

Thank You, Creator God, for the blessings that come from dirt and other unexpected sources.

Words to Pray On

Then God said, "I give you every seed-bearing plant on the face of the whole earth and every tree that has fruit with seed in it. They will be yours for food. And to all the beasts of the earth and all the birds in the sky and all the creatures that move along the ground—everything that has the breath of life in it—I give every green plant for food." And it was so. God saw all that He had made, and it was very good.
—Genesis 1:29–31 (NIV)

The whole earth is filled with awe at your wonders; where morning dawns, where evening fades, you call forth songs of joy.

—Psalm 65:8 (NIV)

day 84

whimsical

Yesterday it was 80 degrees. This morning, snow fell. "Seriously, God? Snow?" As I stared out at the snow-covered jonquils, my heart filled with laughter. I was created in my Father's image, and He has given me laughter, humor, whimsy, and happiness. Our God is blissful and joyful. He fills us with these attributes to help us enjoy His creation. God is curious and playful. There are times He plays with His children, bringing cheer—showing us His humor and the wonder in His peppering us with snow.

Laughter filled me, and I prayed, "Show me Your whimsical ways, that I might find the great joy and delight You bring." Pray for whimsical, and God will show you great happiness.

—Cindy K. Sproles

Lord, show us Your whimsical ways. Laugh with us.

Words to Pray On

But the fruit of the Spirit is love, joy, peace, forbearance, kindness, goodness, faithfulness, gentleness and self-control.

—Galatians 5:22–23 (NIV)

To him who is able to keep you from stumbling and to present you before his glorious presence without fault and with great joy—to the only God our Savior be glory, majesty, power and authority, through Jesus Christ our Lord, before all ages, now and forevermore!

—Jude 1:24–25 (NIV)

He will yet fill your mouth with laughter and your lips with shouts of joy.

—Job 8:21 (NIV)

We really feel happier when things look bleak. Hope is endurance. Hope is holding on and going on and trusting in the Lord.
—Michael Novak

day 85

good

Why did I turn on that show? What am I scrolling on my phone? Oh, the time I've given to things I knew weren't good for my soul, and felt the anxious thoughts fill my mind. But then I hear the gentle whisper of the words from the letter to the Philippians, "Whatever is lovely, whatever is good…"

It's been easy to share this verse with my kids when their thoughts become stuck, but do I do the same for myself? I need to turn off the negative and tune in to the good—a new sunrise, a short walk outside, flowers blooming, sending a text of encouragement, time in prayer, singing songs…there is good to be found! I need to remember to look for it, even in the darkness and hard times. Spending time reflecting on what's good is a choice I have to make for myself. Every time I do, my heart is lifted.

—Laura Ann Miller

Dear God, thank You for all the good You fill my life with. Help me see it in each day You give. Amen.

Words to Pray On

Finally, brothers and sisters, fill your minds with beauty and truth. Meditate on whatever is honorable, whatever is right, whatever is pure, whatever is lovely, whatever is good, whatever is virtuous and praiseworthy.
—Philippians 4:8 (VOICE)

Crowds of disheartened people ask, "Who can show us what is good?" Let Your brilliant face shine upon us, O Eternal One, that we may know the undeniable answer. You have filled me with joy, and happiness has risen in my heart, great delight and unrivaled joy, even more than when bread abounds and wine flows freely.
—Psalm 4:6–7 (VOICE)

day 86

among

I walked up to registration that first day of Bible study. I had arrived alone and didn't know anyone. The woman at the check-in greeted me with a smile and handed me a study guide, then invited me to join her group. She brought me to the table where the rest of her friends had gathered, all strangers to me. But the leader encouraged me to sit among these welcoming faces. Among friends.

Among speaks of belonging, of company, of community, and of the knowledge that we have God in our midst. Whether we are alone or with others, God remains among us. *Among* also encourages us to welcome everyone we meet. To remember that God accompanies us into every situation—a constant comfort, especially in the unfamiliar moments. *Among* becomes a beautiful reminder of God's presence with us.

—Susan Brehmer

Lord, help me remember You dwell among us. Amen.

Words to Pray On

Then have them make a sanctuary for me, and I will dwell among them.

—Exodus 25:8 (NIV)

Dear friends, let us love one another, for love comes from God. Everyone who loves has been born of God and knows God. Whoever does not love does not know God, because God is love. This is how God showed his love among us: He sent his one and only Son into the world that we might live through him.... Dear friends, since God so loved us, we also ought to love one another. No one has ever seen God; but if we love one another, God lives in us and his love is made complete in us.

—1 John 4:7–12 (NIV)

day 87

air

I breathe in the air. Then I close my eyes and listen. In the distance, an eighteen-wheeler roars by on Main Street. One block away, Roscoe, an elderly black Lab, barks behind his wooden fence. In our giant live oaks, northern cardinals call *purty purty purty*. I breathe out the air. Then I open my eyes and survey our yard. A fox squirrel scampers down an oak limb. At our bird feeder, a male house finch cracks a sunflower seed. In the wood oats, Prima, our blue-eyed calico, snoozes, concealed within her grassy den. I breathe in the air. Then I smile. Because I am so very blessed.
—Sheryl Smith-Rodgers

I praise You, my Lord, for sweet air and the privilege of living in Your world.

Words to Pray On

The Lord will comfort Israel again and have pity on her ruins. Her desert will blossom like Eden, her barren wilderness like the garden of the Lord. Joy and gladness will be found there. Songs of thanksgiving will fill the air.

—Isaiah 51:3 (NLT)

Then, together with them, we who are still alive and remain on the earth will be caught up in the clouds to meet the Lord in the air. Then we will be with the Lord forever.

—1 Thessalonians 4:17 (NLT)

For the life of every living thing is in his hand, and the breath of every human being.

—Job 12:10 (NLT)

day 88

caring

Caring for an ailing mother was harder than anything I'd ever done. Tears flowed. Guilt followed. Overworked, I toyed with the idea of hiring help, but we were living a frugal life. *Still,* I thought, *if only someone could get her ready, give her breakfast, and spend time with her once or twice a week, it would give me a chance to breathe.*

"I know someone," a friend said. "She'll take part-time, and she has experience."

The hardy young woman my friend recommended was a godsend. A blessing from above. And within our budget. I laughed, thinking, *Of course, would God provide anything less?* Never!

Gratitude washed through me. I could breathe again.

—Pamela Hirson

Lord, help me to never give up, always trusting in Your provision. Amen.

Words to Pray On

And let us not be weary in well doing: for in due season we shall reap, if we faint not. As we have therefore opportunity, let us do good unto all men, especially unto them who are of the household of faith.
—Galatians 6:9–10 (KJV)

But a certain Samaritan, as he journeyed, came where he was: and when he saw him, he had compassion on him, and went to him, and bound up his wounds, pouring in oil and wine, and set him on his own beast, and brought him to an inn, and took care of him. And on the morrow when he departed, he took out two pence, and gave them to the host, and said unto him, Take care of him; and whatsoever thou spendest more, when I come again, I will repay thee.
—Luke 10:33–35 (KJV)

day 89

singing

Zephaniah 3:17 (see opposite page) has taken on new meaning to me since my granddaughter was born. I take great delight in connecting with her through singing. I love to be in relationship with her, whether she is crying or she responds with cooing and a smile. It's so fun, too, to see my hubby take delight in his granddaughter by humming to her.

I love how God is my Mighty Warrior who saves and takes great delight in me. And I am so thankful that in His love, He will not rebuke me, but will rejoice over me with singing, whether I'm crying or smiling. He sings to comfort, and to heal my broken heart; He sings with me during times of rejoicing.

—Sharon J. Morris

Thank You, Heavenly Father, that You desire a relationship with me, and that You rejoice over me with singing. Amen.

Words to Pray On

The Lord your God is with you, the Mighty Warrior who saves. He will take great delight in you; in his love he will no longer rebuke you, but will rejoice over you with singing.

—Zephaniah 3:17 (NIV)

Let the message of Christ dwell among you richly as you teach and admonish one another with all wisdom through psalms, hymns, and songs from the Spirit, singing to God with gratitude in your hearts. And whatever you do, whether in word or deed, do it all in the name of the Lord Jesus, giving thanks to God the Father through him.

—Colossians 3:16–17 (NIV)

day 90

understory

Walking through the redwood forest, I'm awed by the height and breadth of the trees. Yet it's not only the ones stretching hundreds of feet high that demand my admiration, but also those that have fallen. Trunks fifteen feet in diameter lie across the forest floor and become "nursery trees." From the decaying trunks grow new saplings.

Much like a great story, a forest has layers. These sapling trees and their host trunks make up the understory beneath a breathtaking canopy of still-standing redwoods.

I can feel like the fallen trees. My dreams, motivation, and optimism buckle beneath life's burdens and collapse. Yet fresh saplings remind me that a fall is not the end of a story. I search for nursery trees in my life—places that feel hopeless—and watch for God's restoring hand. Like water saturating the forest floor, His hope replenishes my soul. The understory of my life becomes a living testimony of God bringing new growth.

— Eryn Lynum

Dear Lord, like the understory of a forest, You are bringing new life to my soul. Restore my spirit by Your tender care. Amen.

Words to Pray On

For there is hope for a tree, if it be cut down, that it will sprout again, and that its shoots will not cease. Though its root grow old in the earth, and its stump die in the soil, yet at the scent of water it will bud and put out branches like a young plant.

—Job 14:7–9 (ESV)

And the God of all grace, who called you to his eternal glory in Christ, after you have suffered a little while, will himself restore you and make you strong, firm and steadfast.

—1 Peter 5:10 (NIV)

Therefore we do not lose heart. Though outwardly we are wasting away, yet inwardly we are being renewed day by day.

—2 Corinthians 4:16 (NIV)

day 91

forward

Restless and at a career crossroads, I woke up recently to this text from a friend: "No turning back."

She knew.

Feeling tempted to hang up my dreams—because isn't it foolish to start over with new career goals in my fifties?—I needed those three words. The gravitational pull of my familiar, former corporate career was pulling me back in.

Many people in the Bible looked back. The Israelites wanted to go back to being slaves in Egypt. The Galatians reverted to the "weak and miserable principles" they lived by before they knew God. And Lot's wife turned into a pillar of salt!

Lack of hope makes us look back. I want to be forward-fixed. When I'm invited by God to do something, I want to be like Elisha and burn the "plows"—my familiar way of doing things—and go forward courageously with hope in Him. Who's coming?

—Laurie Davies

Lord, when You invite us forward, help us walk with bravery and abandon. Amen.

Words to Pray On

So Elijah went from there and found Elisha son of Shaphat. He was plowing with twelve yoke of oxen...[Elisha] took his yoke of oxen and slaughtered them. He burned the plowing equipment to cook the meat and gave it to the people, and they ate. Then he set out to follow Elijah and become his servant.
—1 Kings 19:19, 21 (NIV)

Who is this, robed in splendor, striding forward in the greatness of his strength? "It is I, proclaiming victory, mighty to save."
—Isaiah 63:1 (NIV)

No one who puts a hand to the plow and looks back is fit for service in the kingdom of God.
—Luke 9:62 (NIV)

day 92

interests

While browsing my homeowners' association's Facebook page, I came across a post requesting donations to assist with the cost of adding more recreational equipment to the neighborhood playground. The author of the post explained there was a special-needs child who wasn't able to take advantage of the current configuration.

I'd passed the park several times since moving into the neighborhood, sometimes stopping so my kids could enjoy the swing, the sandbox, or a game of basketball. Never once did I think about whether the current setup was conducive for all of the neighborhood kids to enjoy.

The request for donations was an opportunity for my family and neighbors to consider the needs of another individual. Within a year, new recreational equipment was installed, and a smiling young child could now enjoy the full amenities of the park.

—Antonette Cleveland

Father, help me to care for the interests of others. Amen.

Words to Pray On

Do nothing from selfish ambition or conceit, but in humility count others more significant than yourselves. Let each of you look not only to his own interests, but also to the interests of others.
—Philippians 2:3–4 (ESV)

And God is able to make all grace abound to you, so that having all sufficiency in all things at all times, you may abound in every good work. As it is written, "He has distributed freely, he has given to the poor; his righteousness endures forever." He who supplies seed to the sower and bread for food will supply and multiply your seed for sowing and increase the harvest of your righteousness. You will be enriched in every way to be generous in every way, which through us will produce thanksgiving to God.
—2 Corinthians 9:8–11 (ESV)

day 93

bread

As a young bride, I learned the skill of baking bread, enjoying the tactile pleasure and satisfaction of serving a hot, homemade loaf to my husband, straight from the oven. The convenient bread machine we had received as a wedding gift languished in the appliance graveyard above the refrigerator.

When our children were young, I adopted bread baking into our Easter tradition. I meditated on Jesus as I carefully combined the ingredients: healthful flour, honey, butter, milk, yeast, and warm water. *Prepared.* After setting it aside, I waited while it grew to just the right size. *Patient.* Then I took the loaf and kneaded it forcefully with my fists. *Pummeled.* Finally, I put it in the oven—dark and quiet. *Peaceful.* An inviting aroma told us when it was time and I opened the door to remove the loaf, risen again and whole. Perfect.

—Leslie McLeod

Lord, You nourish my soul. Thank You for the beautiful symbol of bread so I am reminded to think of You and Your loving sacrifice every day. Amen.

Words to Pray On

Jesus said to them, "Very truly I tell you...it is my Father who gives you the true bread from heaven. For the bread of God is the bread that comes down from heaven and gives life to the world." "Sir," they said, "always give us this bread." Then Jesus declared, "I am the bread of life. Whoever comes to me will never go hungry, and whoever believes in me will never be thirsty."

—John 6:32–35 (NIV)

And he took bread, gave thanks and broke it, and gave it to them, saying, "This is my body given for you; do this in remembrance of me."

—Luke 22:19 (NIV)

Give us each day our daily bread.

—Luke 11:3 (NIV)

_____
_____
_____
_____
_____

day 94

renamed

What does your name mean?

I was listening to a book that asked this question. After doing some research, I was saddened to discover the most common definition of my name was *brokenhearted*.

Luckily, I was able to see it a new way when I followed the next prompt and found a related Bible passage. In Luke 4, Jesus goes to the synagogue in Nazareth, and he shocks everyone when he says the prophecy from Isaiah 61 is fulfilled that day—He is the one they'd been waiting for; the one who'd been sent to heal the brokenhearted.

We are living in a broken world where hearts get broken. The good news is that Jesus longs for us to bring Him our heartbreak so He can heal us. He can take our pain and use it to bring glory to His name. This changes us, and in the process we are renamed!

—Dede Henderson

Dear Lord, thank You for healing our broken hearts and giving completely new meaning to our names and to our lives. Amen.

Words to Pray On

God said to him, "Your name is Jacob, but your name will be Jacob no longer. No, your name will be Israel.... Be fertile and multiply. A nation, even a large group of nations, will come from you; kings will descend from your own children."
—Genesis 35:10–11 (CEB)

He has sent me to bring good news to the poor, to bind up the brokenhearted...to comfort all who mourn, to provide for Zion's mourners, to give them a crown in place of ashes, oil of joy in place of mourning, a mantle of praise in place of discouragement. They will be called Oaks of Righteousness, planted by the Lord to glorify himself.
—Isaiah 61:1–3 (CEB)

day 95

promise

I'm sure we've all had someone break a promise to us. People aren't perfect, and life sometimes gets in the way of what we've said we'd do. Or sometimes our own laziness or sin gets in the way. But God *always* keeps His promises.

This is especially meaningful for me as I sit with two of my children while they wander away from their faith. As young adults, they've made the decision that the faith in which they were raised doesn't work for them. One deeply questions the very existence of God.

It's heartbreaking to watch as a parent, but this I know: Because they both made professions of faith as children, and I saw the fruit of that faith as they grew, God's promise to hold them in His hand remains true. He called them, and He will draw them back to Himself.

—Stephanie Reeves

Father God, You are so faithful, even when we are faithless. Help me to sit with my children as they question their faith and seem so far away from You. Amen.

Words to Pray On

Remember your word to your servant, in which you have made me hope. This is my comfort in my affliction, that your promise gives me life.

—Psalm 119:49–50 (ESV)

And this is the promise that he made to us—eternal life.... the anointing that you received from him abides in you, and you have no need that anyone should teach you. But as his anointing teaches you about everything, and is true, and is no lie—just as it has taught you, abide in him.

—1 John 2:25, 27 (ESV)

I give them eternal life, and they will never perish, and no one will snatch them out of my hand.

—John 10:28 (ESV)

day 96

canyons

One morning, I woke up and began berating myself for something. It was probably something I said to someone or something I failed to do—one of the typical actions or inactions that make us less than perfect. And I thought, *God, I'm sorry that I'm sometimes not the person I could be.*

An instant later, the thought came to me quite clearly, *Like water against stone, I formed the Grand Canyon. I can form you.*

Every day I'm reminded of the action of water on rock when I look out my office window and see an arroyo, a gulch formed over many years from water runoff. If water can form canyons and shape rocks, surely the "living water" of the Holy Spirit can work on me and form me. I just need to listen for it and allow it to flow around me and through me.

—Nancy Schrock

Lord, thank You for Your patience with me. I have hope in my future because I know Your living water will transform me in splendid, unforeseen ways.

Words to Pray On

Yet you, LORD, are our Father. We are the clay, you are the potter; we are all the work of your hand.
—Isaiah 64:8 (NIV)

From heaven the LORD looks down and sees all mankind; from his dwelling place he watches all who live on earth—he who forms the hearts of all, who considers everything they do.
—Psalm 33:13–15 (NIV)

By faith we understand that the universe was formed at God's command, so that what is seen was not made out of what was visible.
—Hebrews 11:3 (NIV)

day 97

play

We don't get a lot of snow where I live, which is fine with me. I prefer a warm, sunny day. In my opinion, snow belongs in the mountains and those who like it can go see it there.

One winter, we experienced a storm that left nine or ten inches of snow in my yard. I grumbled about the cold and being stuck at home.

"Let's go make a snowman," my teenage son said.

I reluctantly agreed, and am so glad I did. We had a wonderful time making snow angels and snowmen. I captured a video of my son juggling snowballs. "Turn the camera on Dad," he said, and I recorded him pelting his unsuspecting dad, who was shoveling the driveway. We all laughed and played for over an hour, and it felt like heaven.

—Linda L. Kruschke

Lord, help us to maintain the playful heart of a child, in expectation of the day when our toil on earth is through. Amen.

Words to Pray On

Sing joyfully to the LORD, you righteous; it is fitting for the upright to praise him. Praise the LORD with the harp; make music to him on the ten-stringed lyre. Sing to him a new song; play skillfully, and shout for joy.
—Psalm 33:1–3 (NIV)

This is what the LORD says: "I will return to Zion and dwell in Jerusalem.... Once again men and women of ripe old age will sit in the streets of Jerusalem, each of them with cane in hand because of their age. The city streets will be filled with boys and girls playing there."
—Zechariah 8:3–5 (NIV)

day 98

enemies

During the pandemic, I found myself in a situation where the work I did came under scrutiny by a local political group. Whether or not their intent was to target me in particular, the way they focused on my area of responsibility made it feel very personal.

Rather than live in fear, I decided to pray for them and for their God-given purpose. A shift happened after those prayers. I had more peace, and I saw those individuals, who before had seemed like enemies, from a new perspective. In the weeks that followed, the direct attention ended, and the nature of my work changed, so the tension lessened. More than that, because I chose to pray, I was able to respond with compassion and glimpse God's love for others—even when I was in a situation that felt like persecution.

—Katryn Eske

Father God, please give me the eyes to see Your love for those who persecute me. Thank You for Your protection.

Words to Pray On

But I tell you, love your enemies and pray for those who persecute you, that you may be children of your Father in heaven. He causes his sun to rise on the evil and the good, and sends rain on the righteous and the unrighteous. If you love those who love you, what reward will you get? Are not even the tax collectors doing that? And if you greet only your own people, what are you doing more than others? Do not even pagans do that? Be perfect, therefore, as your heavenly Father is perfect.

—Matthew 5:44–48 (NIV)

Be joyful in hope, patient in affliction, faithful in prayer. Share with the Lord's people who are in need. Practice hospitality. Bless those who persecute you; bless and do not curse.

—Romans 12:12–14 (NIV)

day 99

persist

"I just feel like giving up!" I said aloud as I limped away after another round of exercises for my aching back. I had been doing them faithfully, for what I felt was long enough, but had not achieved the improvement I had hoped for.

No sooner had those words left my mouth than I heard others follow them. "But if I do, I won't have any hope!" I had prayed for healing and believed God was leading me toward it. Those words were a reminder that I had to do my part, however difficult.

When we pray, God usually gives us a role in His answer. We must persist in that role if we are to achieve His plan for us. What we're required to do—whether it's to accomplish what we've prayed for or simply to walk in Jesus's footsteps—might be arduous, but it can lead us to fulfillment of our hope if we persist.

—Kim Taylor Henry

Lord, when I am tempted to quit, may my prayer of "persist" remind me that as long as I do not give up, I have hope.

Words to Pray On

God will repay each person according to what they have done. To those who by persistence in doing good seek glory, honor and immortality, he will give eternal life.

—Romans 2:6–7 (NIV)

But we also glory in our sufferings, because we know that suffering produces perseverance; perseverance, character; and character, hope.

—Romans 5:3–4 (NIV)

You need to persevere so that when you have done the will of God, you will receive what he has promised.
—Hebrews 10:36 (NIV)

day 100

yours

In the months before my twenty-fifth birthday, I found myself going through a "quarter-life crisis." *Who am I? I wondered. What am I doing with my life? What have I achieved?* This period of self-doubt did a major number on me, and I felt myself sinking into a deep depression.

Then one day, while visiting a car dealership with my sister, I heard a familiar voice: Lauren Daigle crooning her hit song, "You Say."

Neat, I thought. But then I listened. I hadn't heard Lauren Daigle—or very many Christian songs—in a long while.

The chorus declared: "You say I am loved when I can't feel a thing / You say I am strong when I think I am weak / You say I am held when I am falling short / When I don't belong, oh You say I am Yours."

I'd been suffering an identity crisis for months by then, wondering who I truly was, when it suddenly dawned on me in the middle of a car dealership. *I am Roma. And I am Yours.*

—Roma Maitlall

Heavenly Father, when I forget who I am, remind me of my divine identity. I am Yours!

Words to Pray On

Do not fear, for I have redeemed you; I have summoned you by name; you are mine.

—Isaiah 43:1 (NIV)

I have revealed you to those whom you gave me out of the world. They were yours; you gave them to me and they have obeyed your word. Now they know that everything you have given me comes from you. For I gave them the words you gave me and they accepted them. They knew with certainty that I came from you, and they believed that you sent me. I pray for them. I am not praying for the world, but for those you have given me, for they are yours.

—John 17:6–9 (NIV)

Save me, for I am yours; I have sought out your precepts.
—Psalm 119:94 (NIV)

words in this volume

Numbers refer to page number

accomplishment 42
air 188
among 186
angels 174
be 82
beauty 14
because 148
beginning 96
birth 138
bonds 84
bottles 78
bread 200
bride 176
builder 28
canyons 206
caring 190
cast 52
cease 164
childlike 66
countenance 126
cracks 74
creation 156
cultivate 160

daffodils 20
desire 46
determination 88
dirt 178
doubt 58
edit 44
enemies 210
enlightened 12
enthusiasm 16
faithful 100
family 30
flourish 36
forget 134
forward 196
found 56
friends 76
good 184
harmony 72
heighten 140
higher 110
hold 60
if 94
intercession 136

interests   198
Jesus   150
lament   22
laughter   162
letters   50
lift   112
magnify   26
majesty   172
mess   48
music   158
notice   10
passion   114
peace   154
persist   212
perspective   54
play   208
pleasure   40
polish   128
possible   18
present   168
promise   204
purpose   98
radiate   120
redeem   90
refreshed   116
refuge   130
renamed   202

risk   64
seal   34
sees   38
shadow   102
shepherd   106
shout   86
singing   192
spacious   24
sparrow   146
sunrise   144
sustain   80
thrive   68
timing   108
treasure   104
understory   194
unfurl   166
unsubscribe   170
vintage   8
volunteers   124
walk   6
way   118
welcome   4
whimsical   180
wonder   70
worship   132
write   142
yours   214

authors in this volume

Numbers refer to page number

Baker, Mindy   36
Bata, Dawn   126
Bogart, Lisa   50
Bostrom, Stephen D.   74
Brehmer, Susan   186
Chamaa, Rebecca   16, 132
Cleveland, Antonette   198
Colopy, Elsa Kok   48, 114
Craft, Lauren   66
Davidson, Kimberly   98
Davies, Laurie   14, 88, 196
Dewberry, Kristy   18, 136
Eske, Katryn   210
Ferguson, Jessica
   Roach   30, 94, 162
Fernandez, Mayra   34
Frezon, Peggy   104, 166
Gibson, Tina Savant   112
Hartke, Lynne   96, 164
Henderson, Dede   202
Henry, Kim Taylor   144, 212
Hinck, Sharon   82
Hirson, Pamela   190
Hix, Mary   40, 102, 170

Hofstad, Becky   68
Holzmann, Julie   72
Kastner, Deb   6
Kidwell, April   140
Kimmel, Liz   28
Kropf, Marlene   24, 154
Kruschke, Linda L.   208
Larsen, Emily
   Schlaman   116
Lasher, Teresa K.   172
Lavender, Julie   10, 142
Lynum, Eryn   60, 128, 194
Maitlall, Roma   76, 158, 214
McGarry, Claire   54, 120
McLeod, Leslie   64, 134, 200
Messner, Roberta   8
Miller, Laura Ann   184
Miller, Maureen   150
Morris, Patricia Tiffany   86
Morris, Sharon J.   192
Morrison, Tracie E.   106
Murray, Alice H.   108, 146
Pryor, Donna   42

Reeves, Stephanie   70, 138, 204
Rodgers-Kulich, Betty A.   12
Schrock, Nancy   20, 78, 206
Schwab, Penney   178
Shaler, Laurel   38
Shumate, Kimberly   44, 110, 174
Smith, AJ   100, 168
Smith, Natasha N.   160
Smith-Rodgers, Sheryl   56, 84, 124, 188

Snow, Jenny   52
Sproles, Cindy K.   180
Van Vleet, Becky   26
Verma, Prasanta   4, 156
Wallace, Amy   80
Waters, Jeannie   118
White, Kenneth Avon   58
Wilkerson, Nyla Kay   148
Wozniak, Amy Catlin   22, 130
Yancy, Dale R.   90
Yancy, Renee   46, 176

Acknowledgments

Every attempt has been made to credit the sources of copyrighted material used in this book. If any such acknowledgment has been inadvertently omitted or miscredited, receipt of such information would be appreciated.

Scripture quotations marked (CEB) are taken from the *Common English Bible*. Copyright © 2011 by Common English Bible.

Scripture quotations marked (CSB) are taken from *The Christian Standard Bible*, copyright © 2017 by Holman Bible Publishers. Used by permission.

Scripture quotations marked (ESV) are taken from the *Holy Bible, English Standard Version*. Copyright © 2001 by Crossway Bibles, a division of Good News Publishers. Used by permission. All rights reserved.

Scripture quotations marked (GNT) are taken from the *Holy Bible, Good News Translation*. Copyright © 1992 by American Bible Society.

Scripture quotations marked (GW) are taken from *GOD'S WORD Translation*. Copyright © 1995 by God's Word to the Nations. Used by permission of Baker Publishing Group.

Scripture quotations marked (KJV) are taken from the *King James Version of the Bible*.

Scripture quotations marked (NASB) are taken from the *New American Standard Bible®*, Copyright © 1960, 1971, 1977, 1995, 2020 by The Lockman Foundation. All rights reserved.

Scripture quotations marked (NIV) are taken from *The Holy Bible, New International Version*. Copyright © 1973, 1978, 1984, 2011 by Biblica, Inc. Used by permission of Zondervan. All rights reserved worldwide. zondervan.com

Scripture quotations marked (NKJV) are taken from *The Holy Bible, New King James Version*. Copyright © 1982 by Thomas Nelson.

Scripture quotations marked (NLT) are taken from the *Holy Bible, New Living Translation*. Copyright © 1996, 2004, 2007 by Tyndale House Foundation. Used by permission of Tyndale House Publishers Inc., Carol Stream, Illinois. All rights reserved.

Scripture quotations marked (NRSVUE) are taken from the *New Revised Standard Version, Updated Edition*. Copyright © 2021 National Council of Churches of Christ in the United States of America. Used by permission. All rights reserved worldwide.

Scripture quotations marked (VOICE) are taken from *The Voice Bible*. Copyright 2012 Thomas Nelson, Inc. The Voice™ translation copyright © 2012 Ecclesia Bible Society. All rights reserved.

A Note from the Editors

We hope you enjoyed *Pray a Word for Hope*, published by Guideposts. For over 75 years, Guideposts, a nonprofit organization, has been driven by a vision of a world filled with hope. We aspire to be the voice of a trusted friend, a friend who makes you feel more hopeful and connected.

By making a purchase from Guideposts, you join our community in touching millions of lives, inspiring them to believe that all things are possible through faith, hope, and prayer. Your continued support allows us to provide uplifting resources to those in need. Whether through our communities, websites, apps, or publications, we inspire our audiences, bring them together, and comfort, uplift, entertain, and guide them. Visit us at guideposts.org to learn more.

We would love to hear from you. Write us at Guideposts, P.O. Box 5815, Harlan, Iowa 51593 or call us at (800) 932-2145. Did you love *Pray a Word for Hope*? Leave a review for this product on guideposts.org/shop. Your feedback helps others in our community find relevant products.

Find inspiration, find faith, find Guideposts.
Shop our best sellers and favorites at
guideposts.org/shop
Or scan the QR code to go directly to our Shop